New Approaches to Curriculum as Phenomenological Text

Curriculum Studies Worldwide

This series supports the internationalization of curriculum studies worldwide. At this historical moment, curriculum inquiry occurs within national borders. Like the founders of the International Association for the Advancement of Curriculum Studies, we do not envision a worldwide field of curriculum studies mirroring the standardization the larger phenomenon of globalization threatens. In establishing this series, our commitment is to provide support for complicated conversation within and across national and regional borders regarding the content, context, and process of education, the organizational and intellectual center of which is the curriculum.

SERIES EDITORS

Janet L. Miller, Teachers College, Columbia University (USA)
William F. Pinar, University of British Columbia (CANADA)

INTERNATIONAL EDITORIAL ADVISORY BOARD

Alicia de Alba, National Autonomous University of Mexico
Shigeru Asanuma, Tokyo Gakugei University (Japan)
Tero Autio, Tallinn University (Estonia)
Bill Green, Charles Sturt University (Australia)
Manish Jain, Tata Institute of Social Sciences (India)
Lesley LeGrange, Stellenbosch University (South Africa)
Elizabeth Macedo, State University of Rio de Janeiro (Brazil)
José Augusto Pacheco, University of Minho (Portugal)
Zhang Hua, East China Normal University (China)

Reconsidering Canadian Curriculum Studies: Provoking Historical, Present, and Future Perspectives
Edited by Nicholas Ng-A-Fook and Jennifer Rottmann

Curriculum as Meditative Inquiry
Ashwani Kumar

Autobiography and Teacher Development in China: Subjectivity and Culture in Curriculum Reform
Edited by Zhang Hua and William F. Pinar

Imagining Time and Space in Universities: Bodies in Motion
Claudia Matus

palgrave▸pivot

New Approaches to Curriculum as Phenomenological Text: Continental Philosophy and Ontological Inquiry

James M. Magrini
Adjunct Professor, Philosophy/Liberal Arts, College of DuPage, USA

palgrave macmillan

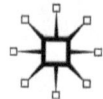

NEW APPROACHES TO CURRICULUM AS PHENOMENOLOGICAL TEXT
© Copyright James M. Magrini, 2015.

All rights reserved.

First published in 2015 by
PALGRAVE MACMILLAN®
in the United States—a division of St. Martin's Press LLC,
175 Fifth Avenue, New York, NY 10010.

Where this book is distributed in the UK, Europe and the rest of the world, this is by Palgrave Macmillan, a division of Macmillan Publishers Limited, registered in England, company number 785998, of Houndmills, Basingstoke, Hampshire RG21 6XS.

Palgrave Macmillan is the global academic imprint of the above companies and has companies and representatives throughout the world.

Palgrave® and Macmillan® are registered trademarks in the United States, the United Kingdom, Europe and other countries.

ISBN: 978-1-137-57319-3   EPUB
ISBN: 978-1-137-57318-6   PDF
ISBN: 978-1-137-57317-9   Hardback

Library of Congress Cataloging-in-Publication Data is available from the Library of Congress.

A catalogue record of the book is available from the British Library.

First edition: 2015

www.palgrave.com/pivot

DOI: 10.1057/9781137573186

Contents

Introduction   1

1   A Fundamental Theory of Curriculum/ Education Grounded in Ontology NOT Epistemology: Recovering the Occluded Realm of Pre-Theoretical Living-and-Learning in Vandenberg, Dreyfus, and Kelly   17

2   Beyond Metaphysical Instrumentalism in Curriculum Theory: The *Poietic* and *Painterly* in Pinar's "Abstract Expressionist" Scholarship   45

3   The Phenomenology of Nature and the *Ēthos* (ηθοζ) of Earthly Dwelling in Jardine and Bonnett: Ecopedagogy, Transcendence, and the Post-Humanist Integrated Curriculum-of-life (*Curriculum Vitae*)   76

Epilogue   111

References   118

Index   125

palgrave▸pivot

www.palgrave.com/pivot

Introduction

Magrini, James. M. *New Approaches to Curriculum as Phenomenological Text: Continental Philosophy and Ontological Inquiry*. New York: Palgrave Macmillan, 2015. DOI: 10.1057/9781137573186.0002.

I begin in an unorthodox manner by revealing *via negativa* what the book is *not*: (1) it is *not* a "practical" guide for educators on "how to" conduct, analyze, and present the results of one or another phenomenological "method" as related to curriculum or education—i.e., it is *not* what is typical in the field of qualitative research focused on "methods" and "techniques" for data gathering, analysis, interpretation, and practical recommendations. I am highly critical of views espousing the potential of qualitative research to address and "solve" curriculum problems when its "theories" are "applied" to/in *praxis*; (2) it is *not* an exegetical text focused on explicating and critiquing the various forms of phenomenological practices adopted in the history of curriculum studies and education in general; (3) it is *not* a self-contained phenomenological study of curriculum phenomena that incorporates the traditional modes data collection such as interviews, protocol writing, diaries, or journal logs; (4) it is *not* a philosophical "taxonomy" that attempts to establish a way of curriculum design, making, implementation, and evaluation grounded in a phenomenological study of curriculum/education, which would incorporate "ontological" principles for establishing the objectives or benchmarks for education, giving structure to curriculum's scope-and-sequence of learning, and granting an indelible foundation, now "ontological," as opposed to epistemological, behavioral, or cognitive, to the educational and curricular experience.

New Approaches to Curriculum as Phenomenological Text: Continental Philosophy and Ontological Inquiry is a deeply researched and multi-layered work of philosophy that draws inspiration from the pioneering work of the reconceptualists in curriculum theory who introduced and established the *reading of curriculum as phenomenological text* between 1967 and 2000. The book seeks to contribute to the rethinking and advancement of this form of phenomenological research in both curriculum and education and is unique in that it breaks open and holds open a compelling dialogue or conversation across disciplines that opposes, confronts, and directly challenges the reign of *metaphysical instrumentalism* in all phases of standardized education to reveal and illuminate a phenomenological form of attuned learning grounded in a reconceived dwelling within the world that is at once creative, spiritual, and meditative. Herein, I approach curriculum theorizing by drawing heavily on the systematic phenomenological roots of the European (Continental) philosophical tradition. Thus, the scholarship manifests in and through close readings and imaginative interpretations of both curriculum theorists and Continental philosophers, which are presented in the form of "speculative philosophical essays," an important form of curriculum *thinking-writing* all but lost to the general contemporary field of research, for as Pinar (2013) laments, conceptual-theoretical research expressed creatively through such philosophical-phenomenological scholarship, "remains in short supply" (56).

The book announces itself as one form or manifestation of what Pinar refers to as the continued and sustained push to understand curriculum in scholarship, and my concern is ultimately with the following: *to reveal through the practice of phenomenology an understanding of curriculum as a curriculum of life in the singularity and communality of its unfolding.* As Pinar notes, in education and curriculum, "*a second reconceptualization is now underway. Through the hybridization of concepts common in the reconceptualized field (1970–2000), a new generation of scholars is consolidating the conceptual gains made during those decades and now complicating them as they attune them to present circumstances*" (55, emphasis in original). For this new beginning or inception furthering reconceptualist thought we need to "formulate new concepts," and for this "conceptual research is necessary" (56). The problem, and this was presciently philosophized by Huebner (1966), is that the language we use, or more appropriately uses us, is recalcitrant—it is resistant to change! This is why Huebner's (1974) phenomenology actively pursues the "remaking" of a curriculum "language that can reveal how the educator has decided to live in the world and what he sees as possible futures" (37). What is required for the *remaking* of language is the re-attunement to the ways we understand and live "curriculum," and this calls for the confrontation with what Heidegger terms the "forgetting of Being," or, as I have named it, in relation to curriculum theorizing, the "oblivion of ontology" in education. This indicates that an *originary* dimension of human existence has been obscured and foreclosed by the attunement of the *metaphysics of instrumentalism*, which is structured by the obsessive drive to privilege epistemological matters over ontological concerns in curriculum and education. The reader must note that although the book seeks to move curriculum theorizing forward in terms of "returning to" the reading of *curriculum as phenomenological text* by expanding and deepening the interpretation of key concepts from the history of curriculum theory, eliciting unique ways of rethinking phenomenology and curriculum by opening new avenues and pathways of thought, it does not seek to "reconceptualize" curriculum theorizing in its entirety, which would represent a daunting, and beyond, an impossible task for text of this length.

The chapters incorporate, in varying degrees of depth, the following thinkers from Continental philosophy who are pioneers in the discipline of phenomenology from Europe and the United States: Martin Heidegger, Maurice Merleau-Ponty, Gabriel Marcel, Hubert Dreyfus, Sean Kelly, William McNeill, Daniela Vallega-Neu, and Michael Bonnett. Key thinkers representing the reconceptualist movement, specifically concerned with phenomenological research (*thinking-writing*), include William Pinar, David Jardine, Dwayne Huebner, James Macdonald, Max van Manen, Ted Aoki, and Donald Vandenberg. It must be noted, however, that Vandenberg is not directly connected with the reconceptualist movement *per se*, rather, much like Maxine Greene, he is a philosopher of education who is a *kindred spirit* of reconceptualist thought in that he too believes in the potential of "existential-phenomenology" to contribute to the rethinking and revoicing (NB: reconceptualization) of curriculum and education in terms that are radically other than traditional and empirical-analytic views of education. I am well aware that this list of scholarly luminaries is abbreviated and therefore limited in relation to the greater phenomenological field in curriculum studies, and this requires a bit of qualification, and so I offer the reader the following reasons for selecting these particular thinkers: (1) they are undisputed exemplars in the study of systematic phenomenology in its relation to curriculum and education; (2) they all embrace, a post-Husserlian view of "existential" phenomenology or variation thereof as it is recognized and practiced in Continental philosophy; and (3) they represent the first "curriculum theorists" that I read during my graduate philosophy studies at DePaul University (Chicago). For example, it was Pinar's essay, "Dreamt into Existence by Others" that first revealed the intimate connection between Continental philosophy, educational study, and curriculum theorizing, and Huebner's paper, "Curriculum as Concern for Man's Temporality," inaugurated the complicated conversation between Heidegger and education that has been the inspirational and generative force driving my scholarship for the last decade.

However, I am not merely drawing "inspiration" from these philosophers as related to curriculum, rather, as stated earlier, I am offering challenging and rigorous readings and re-readings of their works, which have the potential to reveal new perspectives on the ideas introduced to the curriculum field by way of the "first wave" of reconceptualist thought.

Thus, this text does not simply repeat the past in a new form; in addition, it neither apes nor lionizes the past. Rather, the ideas in the book confront, challenge, and problematize the past in order to attempt to re-illuminate it with an eye toward the present and future of curriculum studies as might be found within philosophical interpretations that "say" or articulate what remains "unsaid" in the texts of the reconceptualists while at once attempting to "think" what remains "unthought" in their philosophical essays. In other words, what I am seeking is *another beginning* or *new inception* for the revitalization and resurgence of a systematic phenomenological approach to curriculum theorizing. This marks a "new repetition," i.e., the return to and the interpretive appropriation of new understandings that emerge through the close readings of the texts of both Continental philosophy and the reconceptualist tradition in curriculum theorizing. To approach this endeavor, Macdonald (1995) suggests that we "foster what Martin Heidegger called a 'releasement toward things' and an 'openness to the mystery'"(92), which indicates that we release ourselves over to the texts of philosophy's tradition, opening ourselves in advance to the way that new meanings and unique understandings might emerge through our *attentive reticence* ("silence"), an ontological form of attuned "listening" for what is *potentially* on the approach from out of these texts.

Pattison (2000) argues that when we return to philosophy's past and the great ideas of the monumental thinkers of the tradition, we are not merely conceiving them as "forerunners," but rather in terms of them representing "the possibility of another way of thinking" (135), and in doing so we open ourselves and others to new possibilities, for "our contemporary questions are not just about what it means to exist or to be new, they also concern the future of thought itself" (136). Ultimately, the aim of authentic "interpretation is not mere scholarly or historiographical reconstruction but to think the matter and their thought and, in doing so, seek out what was unthought within it" (137), and this occurs in terms of a "critical confrontation" with the tradition of reconceptualist thought. Heidegger (1968) states the following regarding the interpretation of or critical confrontation (*die Auseinandersetzung*) with original and "essential" thinkers: "The more original the thinking, the richer will be what is unthought in it. The unthought is the greatest gift that thinking can bestow" (76). What I am attempting regarding reconceptualist thought might be understood in terms of Heidegger's encounter with the Western tradition of philosophy, wherein, "Heidegger does not explain what a philosopher wrote; nor is he interested merely in what the thinker 'actually said' in his writings" (Gelven, 1991, 31). Rather, what Heidegger seeks in the *Auseinandersetzung* ("critical confrontation") represents a "respectable form of education," i.e.,

> Heidegger takes his own approach and problem, and under the guiding persuasion of this problem, prods these thinkers with his own questions, reinterprets what the past philosopher had actually said... And while one may not be willing to accept all of what Heidegger extracts from the philosophers of the past, one is rarely left without an immense supply of new insights about the thinkers he has interpreted. (31)

For example, Heidegger's analysis in *Will to Power as Art* emerges from a critical confrontation with Nietzsche, resulting in what Heidegger believes is a genuine critique of Nietzsche's thought. The term for "confrontation" in German as Heidegger employs it does not carry the sense of a "heated exchange" or "hostile argument". Rather, it suggests the coming together of two philosophical views within a "critical encounter." Indeed, this is how McNeill (1996) renders the term *Auseinandersetzung* in his translation of Heidegger's lecture course, *der Ister*: "The term *Auseinandersetzung* (literally, a 'setting apart from [and of] one another') is sometimes translated as confrontation," however its meaning is far less "'polemic,' and carries far more the sense of a dialogic exchange or *encounter* between two parties" (175). Thus, as opposed to understanding this critical confrontation in terms of a "critique" that censures, or critique in the sense of tearing down an argument or position to expose only its logical inconsistencies, Heidegger's critique reveals the thoughts and ideas of the philosophers that he studies in the best light possible, and such an approach and practice represents the supreme way in which to bring a philosopher and her philosophy to scintillate and shine most brightly. In this way the "critical confrontation" preserves and potentially enhances the power of the thinkers we engage. It also calls for us to contextualize our thoughts historically in relation to those we are interpreting, and when we fit ourselves into a historical philosophical, theoretical, or "research tradition," we are contributing to that tradition by "gaining a better grasp of the topics to which this tradition has dedicated itself," and in doing so we potentially further the tradition (van Manen, 1990, 75).

Reconceptualist thought was a movement in curriculum theory-studies (circa 1967–2000) that also included work in psychoanalysis, post-structuralism, critical theory, and *curriculum as deconstructed text*.

I am focused primarily on phenomenology and its manifestation in curriculum studies in the United States, for to provide the extensive international history of its development is far beyond the scope of this text. It was Dwayne Huebner who formally introduced Heidegger and phenomenology (*fundamental ontology*) to curriculum studies in 1967, but Pinar (1992) reminds us that it was James B. Macdonald's "groundbreaking scholarship" that "provoked the Reconceptualization of the American Curriculum field, influencing an entire generation of curriculum scholars" (1). Although the reconceptualists' concerns were many and varied, they believed that curriculum theory in the form of the speculative "philosophical essay" held the potential to change the way educators interpreted, discoursed, and understood education and its manifold processes. Pinar (1975), for example, related curriculum theory directly to the human being's "*lebenswelt* (to use Heidegger's term), the world of lived experience of persons in school, including various modalities of experience, such as thoughts, images, feelings, reveries, and so on" (360). These thinkers were unconcerned with curriculum theory manifesting in and through traditional research, which "tend[ed] to be field-based and [its] curriculum writing tend[ed] to have teachers in mind" (Pinar, 1995, 168). They also moved away from concept empiricism in curriculum theorizing, which has become "indistinguishable from social science research" (170), i.e., concerned with observable and measurable behaviors that can be generalized through quantification. Rather, they introduced "existentialism and phenomenology to the field, in order to provide conceptual tools by which [to] understand the human experience of education" (Pinar, 1976, xiii). Pinar and Reynolds (1992) offer a thoughtful and poetic image of phenomenology's focus in its concern for the *humanization* of the curriculum:

> The firmament in the positivist sky twinkles with precision and rigor. However the spaces between those stars and those hidden by clouds recede and disappear. Phenomenology [reconceptualist theory] seeks to name those spaces, their relation to the stars and us. (1–2)

Reconceptualist theorizing represents "an avant garde whose significance for the field" is to "first challenge and then supplant traditional curriculum writing" (Pinar, 1975, xi). My phenomenological scholarship is drawn to questions and issues raised by reconceptualist curriculum theorizing because they are perennial "philosophical" concerns. As related to my concern, van Manen (1990) describes phenomenological research as a legitimate form of research whereby researchers consult phenomenological (i.e., philosophical) literature in such a way that the "texts" become phenomenological texts for our analyses—*"Thus the work of other phenomenologists turns into a source for us with which to dialogue"* (75). By engaging the philosophical tradition in phenomenology in its connection with curriculum theorizing, we encounter *"material which has already addressed in a descriptive or interpretive manner the very topic of question which preoccupies us"* (74), and such *"phenomenological materials enable us to reflect more deeply on the way we tend to make interpretive sense of lived experience"* (75). The encounter, or *critical confrontation*, with the phenomenological tradition also reveals our severe limitations, allowing us to *"see our limits and to transcend the limits of our interpretive sensibilities"* (76), which facilitates our continued growth and development as scholars, educators, and human beings. Pinar (1991) eloquently sums up the aims of my project through a description of the *truth-happening* that occurs not only in scholarship, but perhaps more originally, in art, when suggesting that curriculum theorizing is best conceived (or reconceived) "as a search for vision, for revelation that is original, unique, and that opens the knowing and appreciative eye to worlds hitherto unseen and unknown" (246). I argue that the approach most germane to the task of "original revelation" in phenomenological *thinking-writing* is found in what Schubert (1991) refers to as the "speculative philosophical essay" (65).

Historically, the speculative philosophical essay was a major and influential form of expression in curriculum theorizing during the late 1960s through the 1990s, and this *poietic* form of expression appealed greatly to the reconceptualist thinkers. Schubert writes of its rise in popularity in the 1970s–1980s within such publications as *Journal of Curriculum Theorizing*, a publication founded by William Pinar. But now, in the new millennium, this form of speculative, conceptual philosophical research, most specifically in terms of the reading of *curriculum as phenomenological text*, has waned in popularity as new directions in scholarship have emerged attuned to contemporary circumstances, e.g., Malewski's (2010) anthology of essays (*Curriculum Studies Handbook: The Next Moment*) that focuses on critical theory and pedagogy, race and gender theory, feminism and queer theory. This is not to give the impression that these issues are inconsequential, far from it, they are essential philosophical, conceptual, and ethical concerns that demand our attention. However, there is something valuable, dare I say, *human,* that is lost to curriculum research with the demise of reading *curriculum as phenomenological text* and its expression within the "speculative essay," and for Pinar (2013), this is a pressing concern. For example, the *Journal of Curriculum Theorizing* has long since moved away from publishing speculative essays and is currently focused on curriculum inquiry and research that incorporates or is grounded in a "mixed-method" approach and studies driven completely by quantitative analysis. Reconceptualists, such as Macdonald (1995), view curriculum theorizing through the essay as not only a unique form of theorizing, but also a valuable and viable practice of curriculum research, which is the ultimate "expression of the humanistic vision of life," which should never be heedlessly "whipsawed into 'accountability' by a set of 'mind forged manacles,' whether Aristotelian syllogism, Roman formularity, factualized hypothesis in scientific terms, or critical visions of someone's utopia" (181). Schubert (1991) points out that

> the essay is a process of inquiry that transcends the problem of reducing human experience to an objectified commodity, a snare of all formal systems of inquiry. The essay, a fluid and less formal form, retains the vitality of lived experience by creating a method of inquiry within its presentation. (70)

Speculative philosophical essays "are shorter than theses; they are persuasive philosophical pieces that use analytic, interpretive, and/or critical literary style rather than rigorous data-based or other highly rule-bound systematic form of inquiry," and, as related to my concerns, they "qualify by most contemporary definitions as philosophical essays" (63). Most importantly, this form of writing is a "special way of thinking" through the issues that transcends traditional forms of understanding, knowledge, and therein lies the essay's strength and power, for it is "not just a way of writing or a mode of expressing that which is already known," rather it is a mode of exploration that invites the reader to "follow along the often convoluted journey that leads to greater illumination" (69). van Manen (1990) makes us aware of the intimate relationship between "phenomenological reflection and the writing process," for phenomenological writing is "closely fused into the research activity and reflection itself" (124–125). As van Manen explains, phenomenological "research does not merely *involve* writing: research is the work of writing—writing in its very essence...The writer produces a text, and he or she produces more than text," for in the process the "writer produces himself or herself" (126). Hence, the process of writing *is* the phenomenological research with the ultimate aim of fulfilling "our human nature: to become more fully who we are" (12).

In addition, if Schubert (1991) is correct, beyond the subjective level, the consecrated act of personal reflection and writing, i.e., the inscription the "I" or "self" in the text, lives at a trans-subjective/inter-subjective, or "public," level, and in this move from the subjective to the trans-subjective we encounter the form of "validation" unique to phenomenology. Morris (2006), in her analysis of Sartre, claims that the descriptions and interpretations contained within phenomenological accounts of the world "are clearly *not* meant as reports of what is going on inside [the subject's mind]," but rather what takes place in the *world*; and readers "are meant to *recognize* something in this description," and it is possible to say that "our recognition is a *criterion of correctness* for a phenomenological description" (29). In curriculum theorizing, Willis (1975) states that the most "striking features" of phenomenological descriptions are the "commonalities within reported feelings and states of mind," and the authors recognize that "phenomenological responses to a wide variety of situations, despite real differences between situations and among individuals, seem to fall within some generally discernible patters that comprise generally discernible clusters of characteristics" (11). This indicates that the *experience* of the phenomenological essay is at once a "subjective" and *trans*-subjective or *inter*-subjective phenomenon: "If the essay is a form of writing that relates to the public space, and if curriculum (especially that preparing for universal education) represents a striving to build a public space, then it would seem that there exists a compatibility and substantive concern and form of expression joining curriculum and the essay" (Schubert, 1991, 68).

Focusing on the language of phenomenological research, van Manen (1990) states that phenomenological writing is a *"poetizing activity"* (13). Language is an issue residing at the heart of this analysis, in fact all of my readings spring from out of the fertile ground of phenomenology's original *voicing* of the world in terms of "poietic saying". Phenomenological language is an "incantative, evocative speaking, a primal telling, wherein we aim to invoke the voice of an original singing of the world" (13). van Manen claims the language is "poetic," but I favor McNeill's (2006) and Vallega-Neu's (2013) rendering of the term "poetic" as *poietic*, "with reference to the [Attic] Greek word *poiesis*," which beyond referencing the creative and inspired process of making, in the original Greek sense, "means 'bringing forth,' indicating a *bringing forth of* and not merely a *speaking about*" (Vallega-Neu, 2013, 140). McNeill (2006) contributes to this understanding when stating that the *poietic saying* of the world is a "'simple naming' (*schlichtes Nennen*), the calling (*Anrufen*) *of* something, a straightforward *phasis* attuned to the *aletheuein* of the *poiesis*...of a letting-be disclosive of world in general, a letting-be that, as enabling presence itself, first enables vision, letting something be seen in its Being" (139).

The *poietic* language of phenomenological research avoids the mere re-presentation of the issues of its concern and lives beyond the limited and restricted potential of the locutions of propositional discourse in the attempt to communicate the immense diversity of the human experience. Thus, the *poietic* language of phenomenology is *affective* in nature and brings to light the "difference between propositional language (*Aussage*) and saying (*Sage*) (i.e., original [*ursprunglich*] or inceptive [*anfanglich*] language" (Vallega-Neu, 2001, 67). Importantly, language in this view is not a possession of the human being; rather it is a gift or bestowal, it is an "inceptive response to [Being's] call that first opens this call by echoing it in words" (69). Moved by the address of the world we are drawn out the "silence," for *poietizing* does not begin or originate with "speech but rather with speechlessness in the lack of the word of [Being] that points to the silent abysmal source of [Being]" (72). Propositional language covers over and conceals "any trace of the occurrence of being [the *primal mystery*]" (75). Whereas *poietic saying* preserves and shelters the traces and intimations of the *primal mystery*, allowing it to be *as* mystery, i.e., "poietic words are able to shelter the withdrawal of [Being] by echoing it" (75), thus facilitating human *transcendence* and the *presencing* that first grants access to our possibilities for appropriation and comportment, i.e., learning in an *originary* manner.

Curriculum theorists and researchers need to take seriously Heidegger's (1968) concern that for the most part we have lost the need, urgency, and ability to "think" deeply about the things that really matter. "We come to know what it means to *think* when we ourselves try to *think*. If the attempt is to be successful, we must be ready to *learn thinking*" (4). For contemporary standardized education *does not think*, i.e., it does *not* think in a meditative and contemplative manner. This is a frightening situation, or at least it *should be*, for educators to contemplate. Based on an interpretation of Heidegger's observations concerning "technology" and the "world-as-picture," contemporary education reduces "thinking" to learning about the world in terms of "abstraction" and "generalization." And thinking, deep thinking, *meditative* thinking, which is philosophically inspired, is precisely what many researchers in the field of curriculum and education in general have for the most part lost, forgotten, or abandoned. Rather than "thinking," curriculum researches, compiles and analyzes data, establishes hypostatized categories for teacher and student achievement, and recommends one or another prescriptive measure for "fixing" the so-called "problems" of education—in the extreme it attempts to, much like the natural sciences, *predict* educational outcomes. Curriculum "thinks" in a *calculative* manner, for as Macdonald (1995) observes, as related to the *oblivion of ontology* and *metaphysical instrumentalism*, "calculative thinking, so central to our society, is built into the very pores of our social skin" (92). Heidegger (1993b) saw the connection between thinking and education and the importance of inspiring a new form of thought, for in "standardized" education

> when thinking comes to an end by slipping out of its element it replaces the loss by procuring a validity for itself as *technē*, as an instrument of education and therefore as a classroom matter and later a cultural concern. By and by philosophy becomes a technique for explaining from highest causes. One no longer thinks; one occupies oneself with "philosophy". (221)

The transformation to our thinking does not simply happen through epiphany or conscious awakening as we find in Sartre's (1989) existentialism and Freire's (1999) critical pedagogy, rather, as Heidegger (1993b) tells us, it is *learned*. For it is the case that we "all still need an education in thinking" (449), and thinking "must first learn what remains reserved and in store for it, what it is to get involved in. It prepares its own transformation in this learning" (436). What is required is a drastic change, a paradigm shift in the way we not only think, but also the manner in which we *meditate on thinking*; this demands a change in attunement (*Befindlichkeit*) where thinking in its essence is not only about a transition in "thought" or "words," but also in the way our Being unfolds, and ultimately, the ways in which we allow entities to *presence*. Vandenberg (1975) refers to this phenomenon as "atmosphere" in education, drawing on Heidegger's understanding of moods (*Stimmungen*), which, in an ontological manner *color* the "intangible, transient flow of experienced quality" (37). Atmosphere, in Vandenberg, is linked with the learner's projective (*futural*) openness unto the world, and these "deep-structures" are "related to the 'affective domain,' that is, to affectivity" (38). Educators must not *flee-in-the-face* of this supreme challenge *to learn again to think*. Meditative thought is impossible to formalize and implement in this day and age where governmental educational mandates such as *No Child Left Behind*, *Race to the Top*, *Common Core State Standards Curriculum* rule the day. These *neo-liberal* utopian visions of a standardized national education believe that student achievement is driven by the best possible teachers and ever more accurate and reliable standardized assessment rubrics. We begin thinking in an authentic manner when we *let ourselves learn to think* from out of the attunement that reveals the ontological call of authentic education and the address of our students. We truly *think* when embracing questions that are *aporetic* in nature, questions that shelter and at times reveal intimations and traces of the *primal mystery*, questions that refuse to close themselves off because they are the most deep and "thought-worthy" questions we can imagine.

Although I am critical of Willis' (1991) reading of van Manen's phenomenology of lived experience, specifically what I read as an erroneous "idealist" critique of "essences" and "themes" in van Manen, we must pay heed to what Willis states about the problems and potential pitfalls that await us when searching for the so-called "universal invariant structures" in phenomenology (Magrini, 2014). This is the problem facing phenomenology in terms of the *fallacy of hypostatization,* or the concern for the potential *reification* and *objectification* of human experience, which harbors the ever-present danger that instead of confronting and transcending the *metaphysics of instrumentalism,* we are in fact engaged in the continued *metaphysicalization* of phenomenology, which amounts to thinking and speaking from out of the very conceptual-linguistic structure giving life to the metaphysical "world-*as*-picture" that we are seeking to overturn. Thus, I tread with caution when approaching the project of conceiving the new "philosophical" task of phenomenology in curriculum: Willis (1975; 1991) states that phenomenologists must

> give up the expectation of finding universal structures in primary human experience. Commonalities, themes, or patterns—yes; structures or essences—no. Individual phenomenologies are unique and can be represented to other people metaphorically. But first we need more and more varied basic descriptions of primary phenomenological states from which to better discern both similarities and differences. (1991, 184)

I offer the following two-fold rejoinder to Willis' concern: (1) in relation to my past publications, I have attempted here to provide new and varied basic descriptions of fundamental phenomena for the reader drawn from phenomenological writings of contemporary Continental philosophers that are rarely, if ever, the focus of either curriculum studies or the philosophy of education such as Dreyfus, Kelly, McNeill, Vallega-Neu, and Bonnett; and (2) I avoid conceptually identifying what Willis calls "universal structures" in fundamental human experience in terms of presentative (re-presentative) [*vorstellungshaft*] thought. Rather, in a far more *poietic* manner, I approach the descriptions and interpretations in light of the understanding of Sense (*Sinn*)-giving/making structures, which are not "essences" *per se* and might be related in Heidegger's philosophy to what facilitates and makes possible the revelation of the Earth, poetic dwelling, *Gelassenheit*, and the four-fold in relation to Seyn, or the truth of Being as such (*Seins als Solche*). As related to my understanding of phenomenological "meaning-structures," Thomson (2009) sheds crucial light on this issue when stating that for Heidegger, these "structures" are really "names for that which gives rise to our worlds of meaning without ever being exhausted by them, a dimension of intelligibility that we experience primarily as it recedes from our awareness," a recession into finitude that instantiates the *primal mystery* (*das Geheimnis-Verbergung*) in all things, which eludes our attempts "to finally *know* it, to grasp and express it fully in terms of some positive content" (449).

Phenomenology might be defined in general terms as a systematic method or practice of wresting from concealment the ontological Sense (*Sinn*)-giving/making structures, which provide form (*Riss-design*) to and are instantiated in the "lived" world. This definition is in no way exhaustive, and it must be noted that the phenomenological practice elucidated throughout is similar in form to the practice embraced by Kirkland (2013) in his analysis of Ancient Greek philosophy, who brilliantly links it with what he terms the "proto-phenomenology" of Plato's Socrates. Kirkland defines this conception of phenomenology in eloquent terms, and he stresses the fact that when doing phenomenology there is no extricating oneself from the original context of the research: Phenomenology, as he describes and as I am expressing it herein, is grounded in "truth" as *a-letheia*—which in Greek is the "compound of a root having to do with concealment, hiddenness, or forgetting preceded by the negating *alpha* prefix" (53). Truth in this *originary* sense is linked with the infinitive form *aletheuein*, which indicates that when doing phenomenology we do not merely stand in the presence of truth, rather we move, because we are drawn into, truth's *presencing* as an event. Phenomenology in its essence instantiates the ontological counter-striving phenomenon of *aletheuein*, i.e., thinking, inquiring, and learning instantiate the ever-renewed revelation of "truth" as it is inextricably grounded in primordial concealment (*primal mystery*). Kirkland argues that phenomenology is ultimately and intimately bound up with the quest to reveal "truth," or as related to my interpretation, unearth the original-ontological sense (*Sinn*) of *meaningfulness*, and

> what is entailed by *aletheia* is a bringing to light of that which is *always already appearing to us*, even though in admittedly obscure or even unnoticed ways, which require of us an uncovering or retrieval via interpretation, refinement, or clarification. We arrive at truth, then, not by reaching out and laying hold of that which was absent from our initial experience or of that about which we were potentially ignorant or oblivious, but rather by drawing out that which was necessarily already in some sense there is our experience *but concealed* or by recovering that which we have already experienced or perceived but then *forgotten*. (54)

Although I retain the original and technical terminology of the phenomenological tradition in philosophy, it is possible to understand these terms in an alternative manner:

(1) *Ontological* as related to *Being* (*Beyng*) might be understood in terms of the *primal mystery inherent in all things*, which is linked with the *how* of the unfolding of our lives, as an ineluctable condition defining our search and quest for understanding—*meaningfulness*. The world, earth, death, suffering, temporality, historicality are concerns that refuse to fully reveal their "truths," and wherever there is revelation within our inquiries there is the concomitant recession of phenomena into concealment, i.e., the *primal mystery inherent in all things presences* through its *absence*;

(2) *Transcendence* should not be thought of as a move beyond the terrestrial realm of our embodied lived-experience nor should it be conceived as related to a transcendent, supernatural, and supra-sensual Being/entity. Rather, it refers to the human's "potential" to become *other* to itself in and through heuristic educational activities (*originary learning*), and such educative activities include modes of non-thematic, non-conceptual comportment or *concernful* coping. In relation to the *phenomenology of nature/Earth* (eco-phenomenology), transcendence is the name for our inscription in the *event* of nature's unfolding with the understanding that participation is always "limited," for the primordial *mystery* outstrips our full understanding of the *event*—i.e., the *event* "is something we enter and are affected by, not something we project" (Bonnett, 2013, 196); and

(3) *Transcendental* is not meant to reference universal, invariant categories or ontological structures of human existence. In addition, it is not a reference to categories of the mind/consciousness or deep psychological structures. Transcendental simply indicates the inter-subjective-ness intimated by phenomenological descriptions and interpretations in terms of what van Manen (2014) calls "resonance," wherein the reader "recognizes the plausibility of an experience even if he or she has never personally experienced this particular moment or this kind of event" (240). However, this sense of sympathetic resonance is not to indicate that we have discovered or wrested from concealment universal and invariant Sense (*Sinn*)-giving/making structures (*hypostatized* "essences"), but rather that we have disclosed certain aspects of our existence accessible to modes of affective thought (over cognitive thought) associated with moods and attitudes that allow for meaning to emerge and that appear to be present and recognizable to us all as human beings.

1

A Fundamental Theory of Curriculum/Education Grounded in Ontology NOT Epistemology: Recovering the Occluded Realm of Pre-Theoretical Living-and-Learning in Vandenberg, Dreyfus, and Kelly

Magrini, James. M. *New Approaches to Curriculum as Phenomenological Text: Continental Philosophy and Ontological Inquiry*. New York: Palgrave Macmillan, 2015.
DOI: 10.1057/9781137573186.0003.

This first chapter is driven by the following grounding/guiding question: Can there be a fundamental curriculum or educational theory grounded in ontology? My rejoinder emerges from a critical engagement with contemporary phenomenological studies in dialogue with the history of curriculum theorizing and the reading of *curriculum as phenomenological text*. Working to develop the notion of a fundamental educational theory inspired by a form of phenomenology emerging from a post-Husserlian perspective, this chapter unfolds in three sections: (1) I explicate for the reader the impoverished ontological state of contemporary standardized education (*social efficiency*), outlining the *oblivion of ontology* and the potential devastating effects of the learning sciences on both educators and students, resulting in the loss of *phenomenological self-hood*; (2) I look to Hubert Dreyfus (1981, 1993, 1999, 2001) and Sean Kelly (2005) to envision the reconceived notion of world and human being that their unique and complex phenomenology offers, which is radically opposed to the thematized and formalized world of contemporary "standardized" education, which is driven, for the most part, by the *learning sciences*. Drawing on Martin Heidegger's (1962) philosophy, Dreyfus provides us with a rich description of the human immersed within the primordial (pre-theoretical) realm of *absorbed-concernful coping*, which antedates both practical comportment and theoretical comportment. It is a mode of existence wherein we literally learn to "listen-and-respond" to the call or address of world and others; and (3) relating to Dreyfus' and Kelly's elucidations of primordial lived-experience, I approach Donald Vandenberg's (1971, 1974, 1975) phenomenology of education to speculate on a fundamental theory of education/curriculum, which finds its home ground in ontology and *not* epistemology—i.e., disciplines related to social science, behaviorism, cognitive science, or neurology. Such an ontological understanding of education, I argue, is to be found, in the most original manner conceivable in the human being's lived-experience as described by Dreyfus and Kelly that Vandenberg understands in terms of pre-theoretical comportment. Vandenberg wonders whether it is possible to envision a form of fundamental theory grounded in the *dialogic principle*, phenomenology's intuitive scanning of lived-experience via reflection, in search of the "essential aim," or the Sense (*Sinn*)-giving/making structure, of education, which, in line with my views as stated in the Introduction, represents the human's primordial search for meaning—and it is this primordial search for meaning that is the (ontological) Sense (*Sinn*)-giving/making structure that gives form to all instances of learning.

Phenomenology, as a qualitative research method in education—e.g., Max van Manen (1990, 2014) and George Willis (1975, 1991)—generally unfolds as a qualitative method in the following stages: (1) stage of gathering life experience as text; (2) stage of analysis, elucidating (describing/interpreting) common themes and patterns of meaning; and (3) stage of suggesting ways for inspiring improved educational practice. Caution must be exercised when approaching the third stage of the phenomenological method, lest we inevitably encounter a problem, namely, the susceptibility to fall prey to two highly questionable beliefs: first, that phenomenology might somehow be able to solve problems, and second, that theory, in a free-floating manner, lives at a remove from *praxis* and further, can be applied to *praxis* in order to predict, control, and direct it. This notion arises, in one sense, because of the conflation of scientific theory and practical theory in education, and the latter represents the proper purview of educational theory, because all practical theory can hope to do is offer speculative and tentative insight into the things we *should* be doing in our practical involvements—*praxis*, it must be noted, is a realm of danger and precarious uncertainty. In relation to the first questionable belief, Heidegger (1965) states that philosophy might not be able to accomplish anything, however, as he assures us, if we approach it properly, with respect and reverence, perhaps, philosophy might *do* something with us—and thus we must open ourselves up to the call or *address of philosophy*, or, as in this case, *phenomenology*.

The call of phenomenology, as Aoki (2005) indicates, has unfortunately been silenced in the era of *social efficiency* in contemporary education. This, for Vandenberg (1975), is quite properly an issue of attunement or foundational "deep-seated, underlying moods" (*Stimmungen*) that *color* the ways in which the world and others manifest for our appropriation (38). We are trapped in a way of seeing, understanding, interpreting, and discoursing about our existence that restricts our vision (as *futural* visionary-seeing). We experience education as a series of problems to be solved, students as products, and worse, subjects in their manipulability, and as a result learning becomes an outcomes-driven activity grounded in pre-determined goals, objectives, aims, and abstracted and *generalized* standards of so-called "achievement". This, I claim, has devastating effects on the way we view and interact with humans, who are reduced to objects, products, or commodities for our use and subsequent disposal. Viewed through the lens of phenomenology, we might say that contemporary education has silenced, covered-over, and occluded the more primordial and ontological aspects of our Being. Herein, I offer educators a vista into what phenomenology *might* be able to show us or "bring forth" in order to inspire us to rethink and reassess the modes of learning that we tend to privilege (especially in the United States) in various standardized versions of education that we have inherited from the tradition of scientific management as it moves through behavioral psychology and cognitive psychology and now lives as the learning sciences (Schiro, 2009; Bransford, 2000; Kliebard, 2004; Taubman, 2009; Jensen, 2005). Many years ago, Vandenberg (1971) formulated the problem we still confront as educators in the era of standardization, NCLB, Common Core State Standards (STEM) curriculum, and the "scripted" curriculum. He explains that "schooling in the post-Sputnik decade" emerged as a manifestation of "the forgetfulness of being"—because schools were largely manifestations of "the blind, technological mentality that calculates what it wants and then manipulates objects and people...in order to obtain what it wants" (131).

The occluded ontology in contemporary "standardized" curriculum

Taubman (2009) identifies two problems emerging from contemporary standardized education, which he traces to the effects of contemporary learning theory, or the *science of learning*: (1) the erroneous conception of school-as-environment, where education is thought to unfold according to the predictable logic of the continuum of *organism-environment-stimuli-response*, wherein learning occurs when there is an observable and demonstrable change in the student's behavior, and (2) the issue of curriculum content in education: it is the case that in contemporary schools the actual content, or subject-matter, of learning in the curriculum is reducible to strategies-of-learning, e.g., the rise in *metacognition*, which is expressed in terms of strategies through which students learn about the operations of the mind along with ways to control those operations in order that they might be "applied" to the various tasks across the curriculum. Examining these issues I show how a phenomenological perspective might contribute to rethinking and *reconceptualizing* the way we interpret, understand, and discourse, not only about education, curriculum, and the students in our classrooms, but also the way in which we conceive ourselves and other human beings. As I examine *social efficiency* in education, I ask the reader to keep the following query in mind: How are we conceiving the human being in contemporary standardized education, and does this view do violence to *who* we are as *phenomenological subjects*? It is my view that since education and curriculum continue to be swayed by the findings of the "science of learning," there exists the false and pernicious belief that when the correct method is employed, through either a naturalist model or computational-computerized model—either environmental or neuronal—that education has predictable outcomes.

To begin with the first concern, the understanding of the learning environment in education is taken from biology: in straightforward terms, environment is the context within which stimuli and organisms interact. Inside the learning environment the learning transpires, and learning here, as indicated earlier, means that educators are choosing and introducing the most appropriate stimuli to elicit or induce the so-called correct behavior or desired outcome. In contemporary education in the United States, the environment assumes a reality that lives at a remove from human meaning, because it is external to the subject. The so-called *classroom environment* is representative of an "object that exists as a knowable space outside the subjectivities of those who occupy it" (Taubman, 2009, 173). Immediately, a phenomenological concern arises: There is a marked difference, not only in quality, but more importantly, in *type*, between the behaviorist view of the human subject and the human subject as it is conceived in existential-phenomenology. Thus, it is possible to envision a limited and stultifying view of the human being, which *social efficiency* in education is producing, set within the metaphysics of dualism, conceived in terms of a biological entity. The contemporary student is reduced to an organism within an environment, or "locus of external stimuli—rewards and punishments—that [can] be studied, categorized, and controlled" (172). As indicated, the organism exists within the environment, but is separate from it, and thus the environment can be studied apart from the organism "as well as in terms of the effects it [has] on the organism," and ultimately, "those effects [are] read in the behaviors of the organism" (171). Since this understanding of environment and organism already presupposes a Cartesian dualist metaphysics with a very specific view of the mind, the learning sciences attempt to "address the dualism of such a concept of environment by positing a 'third space' that joins the two, the space of the mental representation and the inscription of those representations at the neuronal level" (172–173).

This brings us to our second concern: The learning sciences define learning in terms of "retention, retrieval, and the transmission and transfer of pre-determined skills, disposition or knowledge" (183). One of the assumptions of the learning sciences about learning, which is of concern for the phenomenology of education, is that the "content of learning is learning itself," that is, as opposed to authentic curriculum subject-matter, "learning strategies, thinking skills, critical thinking, decision making skills, and adaptive expertise, all of which are often grouped under metacognitive strategies, become the content" (185). *Metacognitive* skills are important to the learning sciences because they provide *thought-templates* that are transposable, for the skills and strategies are portable from context to context. *Metacognitive* knowledge is really a problem-solving model for thinking, and includes "knowledge of general strategies that may be used for different tasks, the conditions under which those strategies may be used, the extent to which the strategies are effective" (Anderson & Krathwohl, 2001, 43). *Metacognitive* strategies are useful, according to Anderson and Krathwohl, in that they allow students to "structure their cognition (e.g., set subgoals), monitor their cognition (e.g., ask themselves questions as they read a piece of text, check their answer to a math problem), and regulate their cognition (e.g., re-read something they don't understand, go back and 'repair' their calculating mistake in a math problem)" (56). As stated, according to Taubman, for the most part, *metacognitive* strategies are now emphasized above content knowledge when preparing students for standardized tests, and this holds true from the elementary grades to college entrance/admissions examinations. Here the human is reduced to an information processing unit within which knowledge is stored, retrieved, transmitted, and applied when needed to the problems it encounters, marshaled through the application of *metacognitive* strategies for thinking (Bransford, 2000). This view presupposes that the human is primarily directed toward its world in terms of a knowing and calculating mind, a tightly ordered neural-web of information/data. So-called *knowledge* of the world, in the form of mental representations, occurs when the *external* world is assimilated *internally* by the mind, and this knowledge is then expressed in the form of propositional (apodictic) discourse—in this view, the *Correspondence Model of Truth*, the "'locus' of truth is assertion (judgment)" and the so-called "essence of truth lies in the 'agreement' of the judgment with the object" (Heidegger, 1962, 257/214).

All educators are familiar with the *scientific method* as a problem-solving strategy, which is grounded in a theoretical (*representationalist*) view of comportment. By means of working through the various stages of this method, our interaction with the world, or the curriculum, achieves a sense of continuity. We might envision this method unfolding in five stages: (1) we confront a problem that interrupts the flow of practice, and we are forced to think in a reflective manner about it; (2) we identify the structures unique to the problem, which leads to the *Statement of the Problem*; (3) we work through hypothetical ideas as virtual rehearsals for action and form a hypothesis, a predictive theoretical construction, which is grounded in the problematic; (4) the hypothesis is analyzed so that its possible, probable, and desired outcomes result from its implementation; and (5) the hypothesis is "enacted and the character of the problem is changed. If the plans for action have been wisely and realistically formulated, then the consequences produced are the ones anticipated; the hypothesis is warranted—it has paid off" (Brosio, 2000, 130). When implementing this method, a person's behavior is intelligent when the action is aligned with the possible anticipated consequences. A good education lives in the "reflection that helps make inevitable occurrences and/or changed conditions beneficial to s/he who must undergo them," for it is "experience, intelligence, and education that are to be understood as comparative mastery over problematic situations" (132).

Regarding the initial problems Taubman (2009) brought to our attention, it is possible to state that the scientific method, although touted as an active, experientially involved form of problem-based learning (PBL), is yet another *theory* of and *strategy* for learning that works primarily by means of abstracting concepts that are applied to various practical situations with the goal of affording the practitioner mastery over his/her *environment*. When employing this method for solving problems, working through the stages outlined earlier, it is noted that stages (1) through (4) have the practitioner abstracting from the "lived experience" of the situation to conceptualize (hypothesize/theorize) proposed solutions, in terms of "thought experiments," which are then, in stage (5) applied, or enacted, in practice to change the circumstances of the environment and (potentially) overcome problems impeding the learning process. This method for problem solving might be classified in the new taxonomy for learning as *procedural knowledge*, because it is concerned with knowledge of how to do something in practical terms, but what is crucial here is that procedural knowledge "often takes the form of a series or sequence of steps to follow. It includes knowledge of skills, algorithms, techniques, and methods collectively known as procedures," and this includes subsets of subject-specific skills and knowledge of subject-specific techniques and methods (Anderson & Krathwohl, 2001, 52). Although beginning from the student's experience of the world, within the lived context housing the particular problems they encounter, each with their own unique and particular aspects, the mind-world split is still built into the scientific method's account of action as a form of *procedural* problem-solving, whereby through thought experiments and the subsequent application of ideas the conditions of the environment are altered.

It is possible to understand the scientific method in terms of an account of intentional action that we find in Searle (1989, 1998) that Dreyfus (1999, 2001) brings our attention to, which philosophizes intentionality in terms of our self-referential ideas in a causal relationship with the world. Dreyfus focuses on the manner in which conscious intentionality unfolds in and through the mental (and linguistic) representations of our goal-driven action. Dreyfus (1993) informs us that such accounts of intentionality require both *logical* and *phenomenological* conditions of satisfaction: The *logical condition* is fulfilled when my expectations for what will occur are fulfilled. The *phenomenological condition* requires that the logical conditions for satisfaction "must be represented in the mind, i.e., that they must be structures of a conscious subject separate from, and standing over-against an object" (Dreyfus, 1993, 3). There are also two conditions for a bodily movement to qualify as an action: first, the mental representation of a goal must extend throughout the action playing a "continual causal role in shaping the action" (4); this is the "intention in action," and is different than the prior intention, which is the goal as it is represented before the initiation of movement, and second, the causal connection between the intention in action and the bodily movements must be experienced by the subject. If we connect this analysis and conception of intentional action with the unfolding of the scientific method, then it is possible to understand the claim from above, namely, that the *scientific method is driven by a view of the human and the world that retains the Cartesian split between mind (subject) and world (object)*, and, as with all dualist thought, there is a tendency to privilege one of the terms in the polar hierarchy between mind and matter, and the judgment here, is in favor of the mind. The scientific method is a theoretical strategy for solving problems, which is mediated by mental representations, rules, steps and stages, and intentional (eidetic) content that is abstracted from the context of lived worldly involvement, and while this is not to indicate that it is devoid of *instrumental* value, it is, for the reasons stated, a *derivative* mode of disclosure and comportment.

Dreyfus' philosophy demonstrates that we inhabit the world in a multiplicity of ways and that we cannot be reduced primarily to an entity that draws ideas from and brings them to bear upon an external reality. This phenomenological understanding might be related to the *reconceptualization* of our contemporary educational practices. For example, the new science of learning, e.g., Darling-Hammond and Bransford (2005) and Bransford (2000), equate learning with understanding, which is defined in terms of "usable knowledge," e.g., "expertise which is connected and organized around independent concepts" (9). We are experts when our "knowledge is connected and organized around important concepts (e.g., Newton's second law of motion); it is 'conditionalized' to specify the contexts in which it is applicable; it supports understanding and transfer (to other contexts) rather than only the ability to remember" (9). Anderson and Krathwohl (2001) argue that *conceptual* knowledge, which includes concepts, principles, models, and theories, is required for expertise in the academic disciplines. *Conceptual* knowledge and the generalizations that accrue "have the greatest value in describing, predicting, explaining or determining the most appropriate and relevant action or direction to be taken" (57). This form of knowledge is privileged in both the standardized curriculum and educational research grounded in *social efficiency*, which manifests as *concept empiricism*. Concept empiricism justifies the split between *research and practice* and is "concerned with developing hypothesis to be tested, and testing them in methodological ways characteristic of mainstream social science" (Pinar, 1998, 171). Its research findings seek to generalize and establish principles and overarching categories, e.g., the ideal student, the effective teacher, academic achievement, along with attempting to establish general theories of curriculum and learning. As related to phenomenology, it is possible to state that education in the United States represents one of many objectifying practices in the contemporary world, and this notion emerges from Dreyfus' extensive work on Heidegger's phenomenology and his views on ontology and world-founding epochal forces, or modes of worldly attunement. I return to the question posed earlier, keeping in mind the view of the human being that *social efficiency* engenders: Does this view do violence to *who* we are as *phenomenological subjects*? I move in the next section to consider the effect that philosophy has, not only on education, but as well on the contemporary milieu, which in great part influences the way in which the world and others *come-to-presence* for us, in ways that shape our *Being-in-the-world*.

A phenomenological reconceptualization of world and human

The view of contemporary curriculum I have introduced might be traced to the "new science orthodoxy" in education (Howe, 2009) and the privileging of analytic-empirical-technical ways of knowing the world, and, as stated, this links education with what Dreyfus (1981) terms *objectifying practices*. Dreyfus (1981) associates this view with technology and the positivistic empirical/social sciences, which explain things in terms of *thematizing* the world within an objective and removed form of knowledge that alone provides us with the "systematic order of all reality," and this is the nihilistic view already implicit to the ancient Greek belief that "the theoretical, detached attitude was our fundamental access to reality" (510). Dreyfus, following Heidegger's interpretation of Plato, writes the following about objectification: "Objectification starts when Plato posits ideas as ideal objects over and against a knower who, while not yet understood as subject, is already understood as something other than the ideas that he contemplates" (510). Along with Dreyfus, educators should be highly critical of practices wherein "theory" and *calculative* thought (*modes of objectification*) are privileged above other forms of world-disclosure and modes of thinking. He highlights five features of theory that work as an ensemble to contribute to the devaluation of the role of the body, senses, emotions, and affective ways of knowing in our *factical* lived world of experience: (1) The drive to objectify the world in thought, wherein the subject is separated from the ideas he contemplates; (2) The drive to make all things explicit through propositional explanation; (3) The resulting de-contextualization of all things contemplated; (4) The re-contextualizing of the things contemplated into an abstracted system of objective ideas; and (5) The formation of a "world picture" that is linked with a specific historical "mind-set," and in the end, "the subject stands outside of and over against whatever it is he knows, and sees it as objective, explicit, context-free, a total picture" (511).

Here there is a move to ignore and cover over the manner in which the human is immersed in the world as *Being-in-the-world*. According to Dreyfus, this leads to the false and pernicious view that the mind is not only superior to the physical world, it also suggests that people primarily live and comport themselves through the use of their minds, and once a context-free world picture is formed at a remove from *factical* experience, our worldly, embodied, experiential practices lose "meaning and authority" (512). In this view, and this is precisely what we witness occurring in standardized education, the human being is reduced to an epistemological subject, and the most primordial ontological aspects of its Being are lost or occluded. Indeed, the new taxonomy (Anderson & Krathwohl, 2001) restricts the knowledge forms in the curriculum and their ancillary modes to the following four main types: *conceptual* knowledge, *procedural* knowledge, *factual* knowledge, *and metacognitive* knowledge. If education is to be an experience of enlightenment and the harbinger of human transcendence, then we must seriously question the limited concern for, and in the extreme, the exclusion of, various affective forms of knowledge such as *intuitive, normative,* and *aesthetic,* which, as Nussbaum (1990) argues are legitimate forms of *emotional intellection*. These affective modes of understanding are far too often dismissed as inauthentic modes of knowing and are excluded outright from the curriculum.

What type of alternative ontological view of the human within its world might phenomenology provide, which avoids reducing the subject to an epistemic subject? To begin, for phenomenology, the subject is not merely reactive to external stimuli, which would reduce the human to a "*tabula rasa* upon which the world makes its mark, a template for social conditioning" (Grumet, 1992, 23). Rather than *environment*, phenomenology wants us to rethink the context for and the situation of learning in terms of a discourse between individual and world, one in which the subject, rather than being set at an objective remove from the world, is immersed in the world and equipped, with *factical* limitations, to freely construct meaning, i.e., "interpret, repudiate, or reaffirm experience" (23). The problem with viewing the curriculum in terms of a biological "environment" is that it reduces education, which we would hope represents a transformative and formative experience for our students, to a "series of reactive, conditioned behaviors best described as training" (23). Although behaviorists accept this view, it is rejected by phenomenology with its avowed commitment to human freedom. Aoki's (2005) phenomenology of education insists that we open ourselves up to the possibilities of thinking and discoursing in terms of embracing a multiplicity of ways in which to experience, know, and understand the world, which he calls, embracing the *either/or, neither/nor,* and *both/and* frameworks for world-disclosure—it is a *perspectival* way of *Being-in-the-world*, which outstrips the limitations imposed by Cartesian metaphysics. This, for curriculum theorist Jardine (1992), amounts to education concerning itself with the "risks of self-transcendence involved in the exploration of many possibilities of understanding, self-understanding, and mutual understanding" (121).

We must note that with this talk, phenomenology is not advocating for the exclusion of theoretical modes of disclosing the world, but rather, as Dreyfus (1999) clarifies, phenomenology seeks to "make a place for a sort of activity that has been overlooked by both commonsense and *a fortiori* by the philosophical tradition" (9). The activity we are concerned with relates to ontology and is irreducible to epistemology, in that *we live the world prior to knowing the world in a systematic manner.* Epistemology is primarily concerned with ways in which we know the world, in terms of *what* it is and *that* it is; ontology is primarily concerned with *how* we are in the world, i.e., how it is that our Being is stretched out between birth and death in terms of *phenomenological self-hood* (Bonnett, 2010). Grumet (1992) reminds us, that if any definition of education requires an understanding of epistemology, "any consideration of epistemology requires an ontological foundation" (30). Curriculum theorists Grumet, Jardine, and Aoki have provided a vista into certain aspects of the human being conceived in terms other than Cartesian, intimating a richer ontological sense of human life than is afforded by Descartes' metaphysics. I now turn to Dreyfus' (1999, 2001) unique phenomenological-philosophical account of the ontological foundations of human existence, which represents the most aboriginal form of learning that we experience. Dreyfus (1999, 2001) does not provide an analysis of formal education, although he certainly deals with learning in his work on skill acquisition in Merleau-Ponty's non-representationalist cognitive science. It is possible to elucidate a concept of *original learning* by examining Dreyfus' phenomenology. It is rare to see Dreyfus' phenomenology in any account of education, and I believe that his unique interpretation of Heidegger's (1962) *fundamental ontology* provides us with a rich interpretation of the most primordial level of Dasein's lived experience of learning in the world.

In addition to *practical comportment* and *theoretical comportment* there is a third layer of lived experience, which, as indicated by Joseph Rouse

(2001), not only underlies the mode of theorizing (*conceptual* knowledge), it is also anterior to the mode of practical comportment (*procedural* knowledge), and this is what Dreyfus (1993, 1999, 2001) refers to as *absorbed coping*. Dreyfus (1999) calls this mode of comportment "a third kind of being—a kind of being that is neither natural nor constituted, but is produced by embodied intentionality that is always already present in the world of involved, active, social beings" (23). The formalized understanding, or the thematized view, of learning that contemporary standardized education embraces stands in sharp contrast to this mode of moving through the world wherein we are already learning in a primordial manner in that we are transformed as we at once transform our world. This mode of existence, a way of being absorbed in the world of our activities, which embodies our response to the "address" of the world (Kelly, 2005), is ignored by the learning sciences, and yet, as indicated, all learning, whether it is practical or contemplative/theoretical is derived from and dependent on this aboriginal way of *Being-in-the-world*. Let us elaborate Dreyfus' (1999) account of "coping" by looking at its structure, which is grounded in activity that is intentional but devoid of explicit ideational content. First, it neither has initial *intentionality* in terms of a definitive goal (*telos*) nor is there intentionality in action, i.e., the holding of a mental image that is stretched out through the duration of the action. It is a unique form of comportment typical of *everyday activity*, a basic way of *Being-in-the-world* that does not involve *intentionality* as linked with mental representations. Second, this *non-ideational intentionality* "is the condition of the possibility of both kinds of intentionality" (2). To return to a point introduced earlier, phenomenology does not want to "make practical activity primary," rather it seeks to "show that *neither* practical activity *nor* contemplative knowing can be understood as a relation between a self-sufficient subject with its intentional content and an independent object" (2).

In absorbed coping there is responsiveness to circumstances within situations wherein we are attempting to maneuver our way through the world with others. One's activity is "experienced as a steady flow of skillful activity" in response to one's sense of the situation, which solicits that person to "get into the right relationship to it" (Dreyfus, 1999, 6). Our purposes can only be made explicit when we step back in reflection from the activity, or, as in Heidegger's (1962) account of *tool-Being*, the equipment with which we are working breaks down or fails to function, which I have referred to as *breakdown-and-revelation* (Magrini, 2009). Dreyfus

(1999) provides many examples of absorbed coping, such as "working, getting around, talking, eating, driving, etc," even though these are undeniably meaningful and purposeful activities, "skillful coping does not require mental representation of its goal at all. It can be *purposive* without the agent entertaining a *purpose*" (7). For example, I often ride my bicycle around the neighborhood, and when doing so, I am oblivious to the engaged activity of biking because I am taking in my surroundings, the *gestalt* of the terrain, and responding, not, however, through the application of the knowledge of "how" to ride a bike, not "through the intentional content of the experience of action," which is a "representation of my brining about the state of affairs I am trying to achieve" (7). Rather, in this particular example of absorbed coping, I am simply, as if on auto-pilot, peddling faster to accelerate, breaking when I want to slow myself down and taking curves with no thought to what I am doing. Although I have no mental representation of the activity of biking as a "bodily action," I am able to perform the activity in a highly proficient manner, all this so as "to complete the gestalt made up" of the situation of biking (6). However, if my brakes fail or the bike chain loosens, I would certainly become aware of my activity and how that activity is related to other activities (a *referential totality* comprising my *world*) that might be linked with the importance of exercise and fitness for my life. I will have more to say about the phenomenon of *breakdown-and-revelation* below.

This mode of original world-disclosure, as Dreyfus claims, drawing interpretation from Heidegger's notion of *ontological transcendence*, "is attributed not to consciousness, but to *Dasein*," in that it is neither reducible to a mind nor a discrete physical body that is involved in the process of disclosive activity at this primordial level (11). Rather, it is the ontological characterization of the human, which, "involves absorbed responsiveness" to situations within which it finds itself (11). Following from this line of thought, this form of comportment that is *non-ideational*, is not merely a maneuvering amid and around objects within Cartesian space, rather, as Rouse (2001) points out, *non-ideational* comportment "discloses things themselves freed from intentional intermediaries," and those things that are revealed are not "discrete objects but an interconnected setting organized around one's...concerns" (2). In the midst of absorbed coping we are not demonstrating "a self contained sequence of movements, but a flexible responsiveness to a situation as it unfolds" (2). This system is not a "determinate arrangement of objects but the setting of some possible comportments" (2). As Dreyfus (1999) states,

"The basic idea is that for a particular person to be directed toward a particular piece of equipment, whenever using it, perceiving it, or whatever, there must be a correlation between that person's general skillful coping and the interconnected equipment whole in which the thing has a place" (11). And this place within which our activities make sense and have meaning we call *world*, the system of Dasein's meanings and relations, and this context (Dasein's web of meanings) represents a "field of possible activity with something at stake," which holds the potential to elicit an "intelligible response to it by a being to whom the situation and its outcome matter" (Rouse, 2001, 4). Thus, at the most basic level of lived experience, absorbed coping is *about* meaning and meaningful activity, which finds structure in the for-the-sake-of-which we do things, and "its constituents are 'in-order-to' realize some possible way of being" (4). To reinforce this notion, Heidegger (1988) describes walking across a room as a field experience: "My encounter with the room is not such that I first take in one thing after another and put together a manifold of things in order to then see a room. Rather, I primarily see a referential whole" (187). Dreyfus (2001), contributing to this understanding of being in the world as a *system of relations*, observes that when I am in a room, "I take the room in its wholeness, and my 'set' or 'readiness' to cope with chairs by avoiding them or by sitting on them, for example, is 'activated' when I enter a room. My readiness is, of course, not a set of beliefs or rules for dealing with rooms and chairs; it is a sense of how rooms normally show up, a skill for dealing with them, that I have developed," or, we might say, learned tacitly, "by crawling and walking around many rooms" (103).

As might be inferred from this account, more important than knowledge of one's situation or surroundings, is the meaning-significance for one's life that emerges from out of the situations within which we find ourselves, and hence world for Heidegger (1962), and the successful navigation thereof, is never primarily an issue for epistemology, rather, it is undoubtedly an ontological issue first and foremost, and as stated, it is related to the way things and others in our world show up and have meaning for our lives. Our understanding, which manifests *as* projection, is always dependent upon the wherein that is the context of the world, and this is always an understanding that is antecedent to both *practical* and *theoretical* comportment, for as Heidegger (1962) states, "*The 'wherein' of an act of understanding which assigns or refers itself, is that for which one lets entities be encountered in the kind of Being that belongs to involvements; and this 'wherein' is the phenomenon of the world*" (119/86).

The world is a context for the primordial totality of relationships that alone give meaning-significance to Dasein's life, and both emerge by means of the relational, or *referential totality,* of involvement, which is a process of signifying (*bedeuten*) through this relational totality the sense of significance (*Bedeutsamkeit*) this has for Dasein's Being (120/87). We are not made aware of the ontological structure of our involvement with equipment and others within the world by means of theories or calculated methods of discernment, but rather the world as system of relations and meanings manifests within moments when the flow of *praxis* is disrupted in the phenomenon *breakdown-and-revelation.* The disturbance, or problem encountered, makes us aware of the function of equipment and the way it fits into the meaningful context of our practical activities, which, as Heidegger indicates, is inextricably bound up with the revelation of the larger phenomenon, namely, that of *world*: "When an assignment to some particular towards-this has been thus circumspectively aroused. We catch sight of the 'towards-which' [for-the-sake-of-which] itself, and along with it everything connected to the work—the whole 'workshop'—as that wherein concern dwells. The context of equipment is lit up, not as something never seen before, but as a totality constantly sighted beforehand in circumspection. With this totality, however, the world announces itself" (105/74–75) in ways that have meaning for our Being and our unique life-projects, which include our unique potentiality-for-Being.

As Kelley (2005) points out, "Dreyfus's approach to phenomenology has always focused on the first-person phenomenon of everyday absorbed activity—activity in which we find ourselves engaged even though we are not noticing that we are engaged in it" (15). There is, importantly, as stated above, at this level of absorbed involvement, a process of *learning* always taking place. In fact, I am learning in the most *original* manner by responding in a multiplicity of ways to the address of the world, e.g., when I reach out to grasp a doorknob it "affords or solicits grasping... without even noticing it is happening, my hand forms itself naturally to the shape of the doorknob" (17), whatever that shape might be. Although I do not "explicitly *notice* the doorknob (ex hypothesi), it nevertheless *directs* or *leads* my grasp," and what distinguishes this level of lived experience from linguistic representations or ideational representations, or any "detached perceptual experience of the world, is that the content of my engaged activity is not a *description of* the world, even one that uses bare demonstratives; rather it is a *response to* the world's demands" (18). There are no strategies or well-laid plans required for approaching doorknobs or crossing rooms. In fact, the absorbed involvement within a chess match in which a master player is involved is, for Dreyfus (1999), an example of "complex problem solving," which only appears to "implement a long-range strategy" (19). However, as opposed to the formulation of a strategy on the master's part, his moves "may be best understood as direct [unmediated] responses to familiar perceptual gestalts" (9). To learn is to respond in ever-new ways to the address and demands of the perceptual gestalt, the world within which our *referential totality* is embedded, and as it changes, so too does our relationship to the world, and this is finite human *transcendence* as conceived by both Heidegger and Dreyfus. To formalize such activity, to break it down in analysis, to step back from the activity in contemplative thought, to return to the example of the doorknob and my grip, the very act of "noticing my hand," reflecting on the activity, contemplating the movement, "breaks the spell that the world had over it" (Kelly, 2005, 19). Kelly goes on to add, and here we might relate this to educational research, all "right-thinking people" should recognize that "sensitivity to the first-person perspective [of phenomenology] is essential to any full and proper account" of the world and human being (22). This recognition of absorbed coping as a primordial mode of *Being-in-the-world* figures into Vandenberg's (1971, 1974, 1975) phenomenology of educational theory, and he describes it as being grounded in our pre-theoretical ways of Being, which contribute to our fore-conception and fore-having of the original experience of *the fundamental ontological* grounds of learning, as manifest in the pre-understanding.

A fundamental curriculum/educational theory grounded in ontology

How might this phenomenological talk of the most primordial way in which we are in the world relate to our notion of formal education or the formalization of the curriculum? Is it possible that its analysis might have something to contribute to our reconceptualization of education in terms of understanding *curriculum as phenomenological text*? The rejoinder to these difficult queries comprises the final section of the chapter. The reader will note that much of my scholarly work focuses on philosophers of education and curriculum theorists from the first wave of the phenomenological movement in educational research (Magrini, 2014), but here I restrict my focus to Vandenberg (1971, 1974), who I consider a major force in phenomenological research in the "philosophy of education" during the late 1960s and 1970s in the United States. His work continues to provide valuable, if as yet untapped, insights into the power of phenomenology to enhance our educational practices.

I begin by elucidating what Vandenberg refers to as *fundamental educational theory*. In Vandenberg, the idea of *foundational* functions duplicitously: first, it refers to a foundation or grounding, and second, it refers to the *phenomenological ontology* involved in grounding the phenomenological view of education in the first instance—Vandenberg was one of the first scholars working in Post-Husserlian phenomenology who performed exegetical work on Heidegger's (1962) *Being in Time* in its potential relation to education and educational philosophy. Although it is the case that Vandenberg does not offer us anything resembling the depth of interpretation that Dreyfus has provided of Heidegger's philosophy, Vandenberg, in a critical and rigorous manner, contemplates the potential of phenomenology's exploration of the non-thematic mode of worldly comportment for the potential betterment of our educational practices. As stated, Vandenberg's *fundamental educational theory* is grounded in a non-thematic (non-ideational) comportment, which informs our pre-understanding of things, which allows us to step into the circle of hermeneutic interpretation. Vandenberg's focus is on discerning for analysis the original ways in which we are in the world and at once always and already learning, or *Being-educated*, anterior to any notion of a formalized system of education (*schooling*).

Vandenberg (1974) states that educational theory cannot be justified by parent or sister disciplines such as sociology, empirical science, or cognitive psychology. This indicates that educational theory is "autonomous from other disciplines, though dependent on them" (1974, 185). Although educational theory is composed of a body of principles that are justified by reasons "related to the findings of the factual, theoretical, and normative disciplines, they are logically independent of these sciences" (185). Educational theory does not possess intrinsic worth or meaning, as if existing "in a Platonic realm of ideas independently of someone's having them in mind" (185). We seek to find "educational phenomena (or facts) about which [we] will subsequently formulate a theory with concepts that in fact do have the requisite logic—and ontological—characteristics" (187). Typically, educational theory consists of three levels: (1) there is the level of practice; (2) there is the level at which educational principles are "formulated within the horizons of the practical situations in general" (187) that are justified by the special sciences; and (3) there is the level that consists of the search for sociological, psychological, and philosophical elements underlying practice; "this occurs within the horizons of the general features of the educational situation from the vantage point of the parent discipline" (187). This indicates that practice is viewed and assessed through the conceptual lens of sociology, psychology, or philosophy.

According to Vandenberg (1974), this provides a disingenuous model for authentic educational practice. When theorists "lose sight of the educational system altogether and explore issues in the parent discipline in their own right" (1974, 188), they give rise to an educational theory that is not autonomous, for it is too closely allied with the concepts, logic, and epistemological paradigm of the parent discipline. Indeed, as Pinar (1995) observes, *concept empiricism* in curriculum research is highlighted by the belief that "education is not a discipline in itself but an area to be studied by the disciplines," and so philosophers, psychologists, and sociologists research and make claims regarding "education-related matters" (171). In this instance we have a theory of education, which seeks to influence and direct practice, but has lost sight of the actual lived experience of education as it is abstracted and generalized at level (2). Educational theory, according to Vandenberg, should in fact be authentically drawing its inspiration from level (1), and through the ever-renewed process of hermeneutic interpretation, authentic educational theory returns to the level of the lived experience of educating with a deepened understanding of the human being and the processes of *Being-educated*. What Vandenberg brings to light for critical scrutiny is the inauthentic and dangerous tendency in education to embrace a theory of learning and curriculum that is "out of touch" with the lived experience of "learning" (254).

As a corrective, and this comes by way of an understanding of ontology and phenomenological-hermeneutics, it is possible to enact the *reconceptualization* of education in and through "reconstructing the levels of theory," and according to Vandenberg (1974), this "requires the juxtaposition of humanistically formulated educational theory and educational practice to retain this pedagogic perspective and to maintain visibility of educational phenomena as such" (189). When Vandenberg talks of educational phenomena *qua* educational phenomena—the *essence, is-ness,* or *Being* of education—he is opening the door to a phenomenological and ontological view of education, which is expressed in and through a *fundamental educational theory*: (1) the practitioner begins at the level of lived educational practice, which is still at this level understood in terms of a formalized education; (2) through the phenomenological method Sense (*Sinn*)-giving-meaning structures are rested from concealment for thematic analysis, i.e., phenomenology scans the lived experience of practitioners and students, and thus teases out those aspects of education that are hidden, or remain pre-theoretical, but are always at work influencing our pre-understanding of education in the mode of everyday existence (as in the tacit understanding of Being in Heidegger, here, in Vandenberg, we encounter the tacit understanding of the *Being of education* or *learning*); (3) educational principles are formulated in relation to level (2) and the justification contributed by the "special sciences" is attuned to the ontological analysis of the structures of *Being-educated*. At level (3) there is already a fourth level presupposed, and this is where the phenomenological method "turns back" to levels (1) and (2) in order to deepen the interpretation of the ontological understanding of *Being-educated*. This is precisely the manner in which Heidegger (1962) views the spiral unfolding of the phenomenological practice through hermeneutic interpretation, which never arrives at a definitive conclusion to its inquiries. For, as Heidegger reminds us, when practicing *phenomenological ontology*, "in this field, where 'the thing itself is deeply veiled' one must take pains not to overstate the results. For in such an inquiry one is constantly compelled to face the possibility of discovering an even more primordial and more universal horizon from which we may draw the answer to the question, 'What is *'Being'*'" (49/29)? What is crucial in Vandenberg's philosophy is the attention to pre-theoretical ways of learning. "Teachers, for example," claims Vandenberg (1974), "occasionally possess great pedagogic wisdom before pedagogy became an object of university research. This is a non-thematic understanding that is acquired through the buffetings of experience in the classroom. When a practitioner's pretheoretical understanding is rigorously explicated by an immanent reflection, i.e., by an interpretive hermeneutic, it becomes *fundamental educational theory*" (190).

As stated, in scientific-analytic forms of educational theory (e.g., *concept empiricism*), which incorporate parent and sister disciplines to shape the view of education, the theorists are predominantly restricted to the investigation of education from within the conceptual lens of the discipline, which is ordered by an epistemological paradigm or structure unique to that discipline, and when several conceptual lenses converge to offer a view of education, the phenomenon of education, which of course includes a view of the student, is splintered and fragmented. According to Vandenberg (1974), this does violence not only to the phenomenon of education, but also to the student, for it is wrong for educators to "chop up the living child into modes of abstraction created by the various disciplines," rather, authentic educational theory should, in the first instance, confront "the 'whole child'" in authentic situations of learning, or *Being-educated*, for this reveals "the educational facts that an educational theory is designed to explicate and explain" (189). When educational theory is reduced to its dependence on one or another of the sciences, for example, from either the perspective of political science or economics, "the direct application of concepts from these disciplines to educational practice has the effect" of transforming the human being into a *political animal* or an *economic animal* (214). The methods for the formulation of educational theory need to be evaluated in terms of the form of human existence it embraces, promotes, and ultimately instantiates. According to Vandenberg, a view of the human being in which, for example, the political "dominates every other dimension," would obviously represent a severely limited view of human life, and in the extreme, it would produce "an obviously unhuman life" (214). The use of the concepts of the separate sciences to understand the phenomenon of education "in no way depends upon the validity of the concepts in their own domain, but must be evaluated in terms of the program conveyed, that is, in terms of the effect upon the child's life in determining who he will become" (214), i.e., grounded in the ontological way that the child is already in the world "of learning" as a human being prior to an institutionalized school setting. No matter how rigorous or solid the science, education is ultimately about the normative effect it exacts on the child's life. There is indeed the hope that phenomenology as it is related to *fundamental educational theory* might contribute to the restoration "of the wholeness of educational phenomena as they appear within the educating perspective" (189).

In *fundamental educational theory*, principles, understood as emerging at the third level do so through the practice of what Vandenberg calls the "dialogical principle," which furnishes "the context of relevance" for *foundational theory* that is essential. Unlike *product-process* models for curriculum making, the principles for education associated with *fundamental educational theory* are already immanent in the lived experience of learning at the primordial level of the student's pre-theoretical comportment, i.e., they always already live in the tacit ways of making-meaning that are not yet conceptualized or formalized as explicit ideas or theories. It must be noted that the use of the term "principle" as related to education appears slightly problematic. Indeed, by using "principle" Vandenberg is invoking the *traditionalist* understanding of the term, and much like goals and aims in Tyler (1950), principles for education are normally established and posited in advance of the enactment of the curriculum. However, the reader must be assured that the educational principles Vandenberg is introducing are drawn out from because they are immanent in the "lived" processes of *Being*-educated. Indeed, Vandenberg (1974) states that when the "practitioner's pre-theoretical understanding is rigorously explicated by an immanent refection, i.e., by an interpretive hermeneutic, it becomes fundamental educational theory" (190), from which "principles" for education tacitly emerge. Nevertheless, I suggest that the phenomenological meaning of immanent "principles of education" be understood in the following manner: Think of these principles for a reconceived ontology of education in terms of *pathmarks for learning*. Admittedly, these so-called *pathmarks for learning* are difficult to instantiate because they are irreducible to quantitative criteria or a formalized rubric for evaluation. However, because they emerge from the level of pre-theoretical learning, they "embody" the components of a thriving and flourishing life that might potentially enhance our contemporary vision of educators, students and curriculum, and they express the reconceived ontological *vision* of a pluralistic human being. This is a being, who, through *finite human transcendence*, continues to become *other* to *itself* in learning and is irreducible to a single, immutable essence, one way of knowing, a single way of Being and being known (Magrini, 2015).

Vandenberg's *dialogical method*, which is phenomenology's intuitive scanning of the first-person lived experience of pre-theoretic practices of original learning, allows what is tacitly presupposed about learning, once wrested from concealment, to inform the principles education, or *pathmarks for learning*. "Established on the ontological level," these *ontologico-existential* Sense (*Sinn*)-giving-making structures, "necessarily underlie every principle that can be established," because they are instantiated in and emerge from our "lived" experience (Vandenberg, 1974, 214). Vandenberg considers and discusses a primordial level of existence that is reminiscent of absorbed coping, and at this level of existence we are tacitly accumulating, acquiring, and passing along information, which is later made explicit in other modes of practical and cognitive involvement. As Vandenberg points out, there is a "slow assimilation of many things that are not thematically reflected upon that slowly develops one's pre-theoretical understanding" (195) and that "pre-judgments are accumulated non-thematically in experience is a phenomenological finding" (197). This might be linked with Dreyfus' (1999) position stressing the primacy of phenomenology over logical analysis when seeking to understand the third mode of being, "absorbed coping," which is "too specific and contextualized to be analyzed using the usual philosophical understanding of propositional representations" (21). In everyday *modes of coping*, as elucidated by Dreyfus (1999, 2001), we already have a tacit understanding of what it means to learn, but this understanding or insight is not explicitly represented via mental imagery, and this mode of tacitly understanding learning, for Vandenberg, must be brought to light and analyzed through the phenomenological description and hermeneutic interpretation. As Vandenberg (1974) reasons, if *fundamental educational theory* focuses on the phenomenological description of the "tacit knowing of the practitioner, it introduces no philosophical, theological, or ideological doctrine of its own, but it does tap an extremely rich resource of [potential] knowledge that is hardly been explored previously" (190).

Let us briefly examine how the *dialogical method* functions in Vandenberg's phenomenology. The *dialogic method* reveals for thematic analysis the *ontologico-existential* structures giving order and "structuring meaning" within our everyday modes of educating. This relates to Heidegger's (1962) view of the task and focus of phenomenology, which means "*legein ta phainomena*, where *legein* means *apophainesthai*," and so phenomenology literally means "*apophainesthai ta phainomena*—to let that which shows itself be seen from itself in the very way in which it shows itself from itself" (58/34). However, this is certainly not to indicate that phenomenology simply sees things as they are, as they come to *presence* before us, for this would never rise to a "science of phenomena." Rather, phenomenology is a form of seeing that *sees behind or beyond* what is directly before us, and this represents for Heidegger, as it does for Vandenberg, the phenomenological move to *wrest from concealment* the Sense (*Sinn*)-meaning/giving structures that gather, organize, and provide structure to our lived experience in ways that facilitate the emergence of meaning. According to Heidegger (1962), phenomenology is "distinguished from the ordinary conception" of phenomena because it is concerned with that which "does *not* show itself at all; it is something that lies *hidden*, in contrast to that which proximally and for the most part does show itself," and here Heidegger explicitly references the ontological foundations of appearances, which at once belong to what "shows itself," and these "foundations belong to appearances in an essential way as to constitute the *meaning and ground* of the appearances" (59/35, my emphasis).

With this explanation in mind, the *dialogical method* begins at the level of observing and reflecting on situations where we believe education or learning is transpiring. For example, when in the classroom with students we might notice several of them having difficulty with a question or problem. These students manifest in a mode of self-showing as "help-requiring". The *dialogic principle* asks the following question: Can we imagine instances of education wherein both children and adult learners (students) do not show up at times as "helpless"? Might not "helplessness," as related to human finitude, represent one of the essential characteristics (Sense (*Sinn*)-giving/making structure) of all instances of education or learning? Can we conceive instances of education or learning wherein people do not require help or assistance? If we attempt to perceive and imagine education without the essential *meaning-structure* of *Being-helpless*, then the phenomenon of education, as it came to presence within our initial observations, disappears; education is no longer present in its original self-showing *from out of itself*. We might also ask: Are there any instances of learning or education that we can imagine taking place in isolation, at a remove from social or historical situations? Since we cannot, the social and historical become essential ontological *meaning-structures* of learning and education. Now, to consider phenomenology's task of wresting from concealment the ontological "aim" of education, which for Vandenberg, represents the "ontological essence" of education as it informs his *fundamental educational theory,* we ask: Are there any instances which rightly deserve the name "education" wherein the acquisition of meaning (or the deepening of the understanding) is not an essential aim of the process of learning in terms of *human transcendence*? Since we cannot, we conclude that the "aim" of education represents the *originary* Sense (*Sinn*)-meaning/giving structure that defines education *qua* education (education as such) in its very Being: "Fundamental educational theory indicates how man [sic] can become a human being through educating by articulating the basic phenomena of education in the structural context demarcated by aim of educating" (211). It is crucial to note that with the introduction of the *dialogical method*, Vandenberg resists the critique of metaphysical solipsism, this is because the *dialogical method* is "the means to avoid subjectivism, for the dialogue is the intersubjective test appropriate to humanistic methodology" (198), it allows the phenomenologist to make important distinctions between what is non-essential and essential, between what is *originary* in an ontological sense and what is merely derivative.

The aim of education, or *original-learning*, as related to Dreyfus' (1999, 2001) interpretation of finite human *transcendence*, is a process and way of being wherein we are always projected out beyond what/who we are at any given moment and this phenomenon is intimately related to "non-formal" learning, because we are always already in the world in such a way that in and through understanding we are on the approach back to ourselves as *other* from out of the indeterminate future; education is an original processes of *becoming-other-in-learning*, and this prior to unpacking any texts, prior to preparing for any tests, prior to passing through the doors of any educational institution. Human *transcendence*, as the embodiment and manifestation of *original-learning*, is grounded in the "third mode of Being," *non-ideational intentionality*, which is not merely a characteristic or trait added on to human existence, neither is it reducible to a function of consciousness, rather this directedness toward the world from within the world in search of meaning comprises the primordial *world-of-learning*, and it is intimately bound up with and inseparable from the unfolding of our Being. This is precisely what Vandenberg explores within his *fundamental educational theory*, which, as he informs us, "investigates man [sic] in his fundamental essential characteristic of requiring education to become man because everything that man is able to do or be directly human is due to his having been educated" (213).

However, as I have attempted to demonstrate, this goal of acquiring meaning is a far cry from the determinate goals and terminal aims of traditional curriculum as we find in *social efficiency*, rather the aim of education, according to Vandenberg (1974), is always already occurring at a pre-theoretical level because "the human is always projecting into some possibilities in the world and future, and this project is understood, and the understanding of the project of being is permeated with personal concern" (213), i.e., concern for our Being and the Being of others, concern for our unique possibilities for Being, concern for the way in which things show up for our appropriation as *having-meaning* for our Being. In this *original* view of education informing *fundamental educational theory* we are no longer focused primarily on epistemological concerns, because *conceptual* knowledge, *procedural* knowledge, *meta-cognitive* knowledge, and *factual* knowledge are in fact all derived from and dependent on pre-theoretical modes of understanding the world as described in absorbed coping. *Fundamental educational theory* opens the way for the essential "accessibility of 'man' [*sic*] in his educability," and this is never restricted to institutionalized settings or formal definitions of education that have been forged and reified within the standardized logic of *social efficiency ideology*. It is only, according to Vandenberg, when we approach education through a "hermeneutic phenomenology," that the possibility exists to yield "educational phenomena that furnish the distinct object of research that is studied by no other discipline, thereby," and perhaps for the first time, "creating the possibility of a discipline of education" (213).

In the end: The grounding of *ground*

Adopting a critical view of Vandenberg's position it is possible to state that it falls victim to its own critique of traditional educational theory—for in place of the disciplines such as philosophy and science, the educational experience is now viewed through the restricted conceptual lens of "phenomenology" with its unique paradigm for knowledge. Why should we accept the claim that phenomenology offers us the potential for a more authentic form of educational theory than the tradition? Is this view not also limited in the scope of its vision? These are legitimate concerns, however I believe the following rejoinder might be marshaled in defense of Vandenberg's turn to phenomenology (and ipso facto ontology) in the attempt to rescue educational theory: Since we are dealing with ontology, we are dealing with the most fundamental (essential) ways of our existence as human beings. Since ontological issues are always before epistemological concerns with knowledge and psychological categories for structuring conscious existence, it is possible to state, invoking later Wittgenstein (1958), that when we reach ground, or "bedrock," there can be no more talk of justification or validation, but rather, as Aoki (2005) claims, at this point, we are simply standing in the presence of the *is-ness* of existence. Phenomenology indeed brings us into close proximity to the very grounds (*is-ness*) of our existence by returning us to the primordial aspects of life that have been covered over and occluded by a technological-scientific worldview.

Importantly, Vandenberg's (1971) *fundamental educational theory* resists the tendency in analytic-empirical modes of education to reify the student, which is the "analytic reduction of the phenomenon to something else" (140), i.e., the human student becomes something other than human—a number, place-holder, percentile, or statistic. *Fundamental educational theory* embraces "nonreductive and nonobjectifying" ways of viewing and encountering the student that are necessary for authentic education to obtain (140). Fundamental educational theory allows for, and further, facilitates the coexistence between teachers and students, which represents the "projecting into possibilities in the world" in relation to the "co-disclosure of possibilities of being" (140). Such a concept and enactment of education, however, according to Vandenberg, is impossible within the "established societal power structures" dictating the "relations between people," which are reduced to "dominance/submission patters, to commanding/obeying relations" (131). Those words were penned more than 40 years ago, and now I must ask as educators how far have we progressed in the quest to overcome the disingenuous binary power structures of which Vandenberg speaks? In response to this query I claim that we have not yet outstripped *social efficiency*, which, as argued throughout, is a limiting and stultifying view of education that has lost sight of and is moving farther away from the human subject as conceived by Heidegger, Dreyfus, and Vandenberg, namely, in terms of *Being-in-the-world*. In this chapter I have attempted to contribute to the further development of Vandenberg's early thought by demonstrating its continued relevance and immediacy in a time of high stakes testing, standardization, and hyper-accountability, where educators still cling to the false and empty promises of reform proffered by analytic-empirical (quantitative) research, which is grounded in the *instrumentalist-representationalist* view of education. Educational reform on a grand scale is an unrealistic hope, for envisioning the mass liberation of education in this manner ignores the complexity and depth of what is involved to accomplish this task (Magrini, 2012). However, perhaps it is possible to open worlds in the current curriculum that stand beyond the technical-empirical attunement of *social efficiency* and its drive for standardization. Perhaps it is possible in such worlds to catch a momentary glimpse of a reconfigured, or better, a transfigured human being in terms other than a cold, sterile epistemological subject of knowledge. This, as I have suggested, calls for educators to turn to phenomenology and philosophers such as Heidegger, Dreyfus, and Vandenberg for the insights afforded into original ways of Being and learning, which might inspire both educators and students to "adopt a richer ontology than the Cartesian one of minds and nature assumed by Husserl and Searle" (Dreyfus, 1999, 24).

The reader will note the following:

This chapter appears in an earlier form in the following open-access journal: *Reconstruction: Social Inquiry and Contemporary Culture: Phenomenology and Education,* 14(2), 1–21. Reconstruction.eserver.org/issues/142contents_142.shtml.

2
Beyond Metaphysical Instrumentalism in Curriculum Theory: The *Poietic* and *Painterly* in Pinar's "Abstract Expressionist" Scholarship

Magrini, James. M. *New Approaches to Curriculum as Phenomenological Text: Continental Philosophy and Ontological Inquiry.* New York: Palgrave Macmillan, 2015. DOI: 10.1057/9781137573186.0004.

The argumentation in this chapter unfolds in four sections: (1) I introduce William Pinar's reading of Jackson Pollack's abstract painting, *The White Cockatoo* in its connection to curriculum theorizing. This section unpacks the crucial difference between "representational" scholarship and "abstract expressionist" scholarship. I introduce the understanding of what I term "*re*-presentational research"; (2) I present a critique of technology found in Martin Heidegger's later writings (the "Turn"— *Kehre*) concerned with science and research, which includes a critique of curriculum research grounded in concept empiricism. The analysis of modern technology sets the stage for the understanding of an age where art's ability to gather and reveal "truth" is impeded; (3) building on the interpretation of Heidegger I turn to Maurice Merleau-Ponty's phenomenological account of art as a form of expression that dynamically combines the pre-theoretical sectors of bodily experience, i.e., the visual and motor field of the artist, who, through engagement with the canvas, leaves phenomenological "traces" that speak a new ("painterly") language that is beyond the technical and instrumental language of psychology, anthropology, or the sciences. This analysis leads into a discussion concerning the potential epochal "saving power" of abstract expressionism ("action-painting") as a form of non-metaphysical or non-*re*-presentational art; and (4) bringing together Heidegger and Merleau-Ponty, I conclude by making the case for the neo-reconceptualization of our curricular practices by considering a philosophical form of curriculum research that lives as an expression and *translation* of the "poietic" and "painterly" form(s) of phenomenological language inspired by art, which speaks *of* the world as opposed to speaking *about* it. Ultimately, I return the reader to Pinar's (1991) "abstract expressionist" scholarship with a renewed sense of understanding in such a way "might support affirmative and transformational educational experience" (245).

William Pinar and Jackson Pollack: abstract expressionist scholarship and re-presentational research

In the brief but influential essay, "The White Cockatoo," Pinar (1991) meditates on curriculum in terms of an *aesthetic phenomenon* to suggest new "conceptual tools for teaching, researching and evaluating curriculum" (244). In this essay, Pinar, who pioneered the reading of curriculum through the inclusion of autobiography (*currere*), examines Pollack's action-painting, *The White Cockatoo* (1948). Through a phenomenological reading, Pinar attempts to show that "representational scholarship" and "abstract expressionist scholarship" (non-representational) in curriculum theorizing represent two potential *modes of dis-closure* revealing the phenomenon of education. The latter form of creative scholarship, with its distinct mode of revelation, gestures beyond the technical-empirical conception and enactment of curriculum. Herein, I refer to these modes *dis-closure* as "events" of *truth-happening*, i.e., ways in which the "world" of our concern manifests in a specific manner (mode of *self-showing*) for our appropriation, which facilitates practical comportment. Madeleine Grumet's words introduce the essay: "The aesthetic function of curriculum replaces the amelioration of the technological function with revelation" (Grumet, 1976, as quoted in Pinar, 1991, 244). This suggests, in line with the theme of this chapter, that the "aesthetic function" of curriculum facilitates our transcendence, in terms of "revelation," beyond the purely *instrumental* function of technical-empirical education. However, it is necessary to point out that both art and technology (as *techne*) facilitate unique, albeit distinct, modes of *dis-closure*, i.e., both represent unique events of *truth-happening*. I develop this crucial issue later, because Heidegger (1993a, 1977, 1996), in his later work, is highly critical, if not dismissive, of art's function as a revelatory "world-founding" mode of *truth-happening*, and indeed, this critique underpins my analysis of "abstract art" in modernity.

Pollack, in first leaving behind his early expressionist painting style, fueled by surrealist dream imagery and Freudian psychology, adopted an abstract "drip" method. By distilling the concentrated essence of a larger whole, Pollack painted his autobiography in such a powerful and direct way that he "broke down the barriers between art and life" (Pinar, 1991, 245). Pinar, in a manner akin to Pollack, moving in the direction of creative qualitative research and away from empirical-analytic research, seeks to break down the "barriers between curriculum and life" (244) in order to support the transfiguration of the educational experience. The analogy between Pollack's abandonment of "realism or representational painting" and Pinar's turn from empirical or statistical research is by no means insignificant, because Pinar intimates the crucial link between "representation" in art and curriculum and "representation" in empirical-analytic research. The implications of this move are monumental, for to associate "representation" in research with technical and empirical modes of *dis-closure* is to understand the world in terms of its *re*-presentation, in that such modes of *dis-closure*, in a reductive and disingenuous manner, *re*-produce the world in terms of what Heidegger (1977) pejoratively labels the "world-picture," or world-*as*-picture. For Heidegger, this view is linked inextricably to technical and empirical modes of *dis-closure* attuned in and through *metaphysical instrumentalism*, with its linguistic-conceptual schema organized around the binary oppositions between subject-object, inner-outer, Being and becoming, reality and appearance, permanence and change. In modernity, one way this schema is *re*-presented occurs in art through the metaphysical understanding of and the relationship between *image* and *symbol*, and it is possible to approach this issue through an understanding of Merleau-Ponty's phenomenology of art.

According to Pinar (1991), "Relinquishing realism allowed Pollack to become more self-conscious about the very process of painting, the generation of each stroke and line" (246). In reading curriculum, the inspiration drawn from Pollack and abstract expressionist painting allows Pinar to understand the experience of art as a multi-sensory phenomenon with "ever changing landscapes of colors, textures, motions, and smells," which indicates that the participant in the *truth-happening* of Pollack's abstract expressionist paintings experiences a *synaesthetic* attunement. This is precisely the manner in which Matthews (2003) describes the revelatory experience of art, wherein "synaesthesia" occurs, for the artist's painting instantiates and inspires the "working together of different senses," which is the "essence of perception as we actually live it, although it is very hard to explain in the objectivist terms of science" (136). According to Pinar (1991), it inspires the curriculum theorist to

> become more self-conscious about the "strokes" and "lines" etched into the personality by the curricular experience (and vice versa). The point here is to suggest to you that the processes in which Pollack was engaged, processes that begin with the relinquishing of so-called realism or representationalism, and end in abstract dynamics of color, shape, and texture, allow us to see anew and understand anew. Such is the high purpose of art and such is the high purpose of scholarship in curriculum...the point of curriculum study can be conceived of as a search for vision, for revelation that is original, unique and that opens the knowing and appreciative eye to worlds hitherto unseen and unknown. (246)

This reconceptualized view of curriculum and its theorizing emerges from what Pinar terms "abstract expressionist scholarship," which he describes as "intellectually experimental and revelatory" (247). When curriculum theorizing draws its inspiration from abstract art it faces the supreme challenge of writing curriculum "nonrepresentationally" (249), which means the temptation to approach curriculum in terms of an *object* of study, as is common in all "philosophy of X" approaches, must be resisted. Instead, the so-called focus or "subject" of our studies must be approached in ways that avoids objectification, in ways that resists hypostatizing and substantizing what is being analyzed and communicated. Thus, in light of Pinar's "abstract expressionist" scholarship, we must find a unique form of language that allows us to speak "of" as opposed to speak "about" curriculum, and this becomes a possibility, I argue, when we understand and embrace the ontology of curriculum in terms of a "painterly" and "poietic" phenomenon. However, as Heidegger (1993b) warns, the danger is always present that even when speaking "of" the phenomenological revelation of curriculum we might encounter the *aporia* that it "probably cannot be re-presented at all, in so far as in re-presenting, everything has become an object that stands opposite us" (67).

Pinar (1991) sets "abstract expressionist scholarship" apart from "representational scholarship," which is a form of scholarship linked with projects that seek clarity in the organization of "major curriculum discourses" (247), e.g., the analysis of historical movements of curriculum thought and theory. However, I am concerned with the form of research that is related to *re*-presentational modes of world-*dis-closure*, a category and mode of *truth-happening* that Pinar links with "realism or representational painting," namely, *empirical-analytic* research ("*re*-presentational" research), which seeks results that are generalized, repeatable, and predicable. Echoing Pinar's (1991) concern with standardized education's "obsession with the 'technical' in curriculum development" (246), Howe (2009 claims that "empirical" research in the "technocratic" democratic context of education in the United States, embraces a "distinctive positivist bent in that it formulates policy by aggregating preferences (values) that are held to be beyond the reach of critical examination" (432). Howe terms the practice of privileging empirical research above all other forms of research the "new scientific orthodoxy," and it is codified and reinforced in the American Educational Research Association's (AERA's) *Standards for Reporting on Empirical Social Science Research* (2006). According to AERA's mission statement, educational research should "proceed cumulatively: from describing and conjecturing, to establishing causal relationships, to understanding such relationships" (431). In the extreme, as the condition exists today, qualitative forms of research are for the most part marginalized, thus educators at all levels are experiencing the *empirical science-humanities divide* in research, policy, and the classroom. This mode of "technical-and-scientific" world-disclosure is an inauthentic and dangerous form of *re*-presenting the "world-*as*-picture" for the repeated consumption of our students, which is grounded in the view of "science-*as*-research" and philosophy as a new form of metaphysics, in terms of *metaphysical instrumentalism* (Heidegger, 1977, 1993a).

As stated, it is possible to link "empirical" or "*re*-presentational" research with a view to curriculum and education that is technical-scientific in nature, which manifests on two fronts—*traditionalist* and *concept empiricist* research. *Traditionalists* tend to be concerned with researching and analyzing the "set of perceived realities of classrooms and school settings generally" (Pinar, 1995, 169–170). Traditionalist curriculum making advances the early emergence of "scientism" and its implementation in business and factories to improve production. "This model is characterized by its ameliorative orientation, ahistorical posture, and an allegiance to behaviorism...and 'technological rationality'" (169). Concept empiricism is highlighted by the belief that "education is not a discipline in itself but an area to be studied by the disciplines," and so philosophers, psychologists, and sociologists research and make claims regarding "education-related matters" (171). This type of research can be classified as "employing conceptual and empirical" methods, in the sense that "social scientists typically employ them"—i.e., "developing a hypothesis to be tested, and testing them in methodological ways characteristic of mainstream social science" (171). I argue, based on Heidegger's critique of technology and *science-as-research*, that both forms of curriculum research are grounded in the metaphysical schema of world-*as*-picture, and thus each perpetuates and *re*-produces a Cartesian "reality."

The point of curriculum theorizing, according to Pinar, is not to produce theories with predictable outcomes, programmatic curriculum schemas, or objective, a-historical generalizations for rigid, a-temporal classification. Yet in contemporary curriculum studies, referencing the neo-taxonomies of those working in empirical or statistical research (*re*-presentational research), it is possible to state, as related to Heidegger, that cognitive knowledge, or calculative knowledge (*Erkennen*), is the primary mode of world disclosure with which contemporary education is concerned, e.g., *How People Learn Framework* and *Teaching with the Brain in Mind* (Anderson & Krathwohl, 2001; Darling-Hammond & Bransford 2005; Bransford, 2000, Jensen, 2005). For example, Heidegger's view of *science as research* is substantiated within the Three-Year Integrated Competency-Based Model (ICBM) for higher education proposed in 2013 by Bradley, Seidman, and Painchaud. All the ways that the authors suggest are advantageous for ensuring authentic "learning" resemble behavioral and neurological models for storage, process, and effective retrieval. The research underlying the ICBM adopts an original "projected" view of students and student learning in terms of the "transfer" of information with students defined as "efficient learners" when they demonstrate a host of pre-determined behavioral-cognitive skill-sets and competencies. According to Heidegger (1993a), the establishment of *nomological* principles for standardized education emerging from such research is always "accomplished with reference to the [original] ground plan [*mathemata*] of the object-sphere" (269), and this *object sphere* is given form in and through the attunement of *metaphysical instrumentalism*.

The technical re-presentation of metaphysical instrumentalism: the age of the "world-as-picture," Descartes, and Renaissance art

In this section, I elucidate the Heideggerian foundations that give structure to what I have termed "re-presentational research" in curriculum studies, which might be read back into, and indeed mapped onto, Pinar's original analysis. In addition, I argue, along with Froman (1993), in his analysis of Merleau-Ponty's aesthetics, that "action painting" (*abstract expressionism*) holds the potential *as* a new form of art to displace "the apprehension of world-as-picture and open possibilities for different modes of world apprehension" (338), facilitating the move beyond the "mode of world apprehension essential to the metaphysical foundations of the modern age," which "were worked out philosophically by Rene Descartes" (337). Recall that attention must be paid to both art's ability to reveal entities and worlds along with technical and scientific modes of "seeing," or the unique mode of world *dis-closure* revealing Being and beings associated with "*re*-presentational research" in curriculum. It is therefore necessary to explore in some detail what Heidegger (1977, 1993a) philosophizes about technology's attunement (*das Ge-stell*) as *En-framing*.

For Heidegger, *das Ge-stell* is the pure *En-framing* effect of technology, which is an attunement linked to a restrictive mode of world-*dis-closure* that conceals the essence of the truth of Being and is imposed on humans. What technology discloses, unlike what is revealed through the fundamental attunement of great works of historical-founding art, reduces all things to commodities and objects that are usable and disposable. Under the founding attunement of *En-framing*, the entire world shows up in terms of a "standing reserve". Attuned by the *Ge-stell* of modern technology, we are driven to quantify our existence, including, for our purposes, educational systems, in terms of pure and unadulterated resources for our nation's technological-economic advancement. It is under the sway of technology's *En-framing* effect that it is possible to understand and critique contemporary education because of its inextricable relation to technology, mathematics, and science, e.g., as in STEM related to Common Core States Standards Curriculum in the United States. Heidegger's conception and definition of "science as research" will prove helpful in understanding the contemporary situation in today's milieu of "standardized" education, which is consumed by and obsessed with empirical research (the *learning sciences*). It is important to note that Heidegger is not indicating that science is reliant on research to be *as* science in the modern world. Rather, Heidegger's (1977) radical claim is that modern science is inseparable from research, i.e., "the *essence* of what we today call science is research" (118).

Analyzing the *essence* of research reveals several interesting things about science, its so-called methods and methodologies, and the unique way in which *science as research* discloses the world and entities in a highly limited and dangerously reductive manner, i.e., through mathematics, or *mathemata*, which is a mode of world *dis-closure* (*truth-happening*) that structures the "evident aspects of things within which we are always already moving and according to which we experience them as things at all, and as such things" (Heidegger, 1993a, 277). Modern research is not about discovery in the true sense of the enterprise, for it sees and knows its ends in advance of any of its practices or methods, and this is accomplished through what Heidegger terms a reliance on "procedure," which is a way of disclosing things by opening up an "object-sphere" in and through a "technical" mode of *seeing that has already seen in advance*. For example, "research" consistent with the *learning sciences* is grounded in the erroneous view that explanatory forces, with nomological certainty, can be discovered which then determine "practical" implications for teaching. "Explanation," according to Heidegger (1977), "takes place in investigation," which transpires in through experimentation, however, experiments are set up to "represent or conceive [*vorstellen*] the conditions under which a specific set of motions can be made susceptible of being followed in its necessary progression, i.e., of being controlled in advance by calculation" (121).

McNeill (1999) develops the concept of "procedure" as related to research when arguing that Heidegger "does not refer primarily to method or methodology; the latter is possible only within a realm of beings that already lie open or manifest before us" (167), i.e., procedure is not wholly reducible to method, for a multiplicity of methods/methodologies might function under the purview of procedure. Rather, procedure is Heidegger's term for the way of conducting research that is bound up with the opening up of a realm, region, or "object-region" in a particular way through a projection of a view of things that is already antecedent to the way in which methods and methodologies are employed. Procedure might be understood in terms of an antecedent projection of Being and beings that determines the limits and scope of the investigation, and hence the methods and practices marshaled in service of the procedure determining the investigation. Heidegger's claim is that this *initial projection* is determined by a view of things grounded in the *metaphysics of presence*, and it is, as McNeill (1999) points out,

> precisely the opening up of such a sphere that is the fundamental event of research. The projection sketches out in advance the manner in which the knowing procedure must bind itself and adhere to the sphere opened up. This binding adherence is the rigor of research [which might be termed the "obligation" for method to remain determined by the realm opened up]. Through the projecting of the ground plan and the prescribing of rigor, procedure makes secure for itself its sphere of objects within the realm of Being. (118)

A unique and complex situation exists in relation to contemporary education when this view is linked to the realm of scientific or quantitative research described in Heideggerian terms: Before "method" there is already a view of Being and beings and general phenomena (educators/students/education) that prefigures it, this indicates that there is an antecedent "projection" of how Being and beings [should and do] manifest that is established through the researchers' "projections of specific object-spheres" (126). So, to reiterate, *science as research* in the *learning sciences* is not about "discovery," rather it is concerned primarily with approaching problems with a view of Being and beings already in mind (the ends/results are already in plain sight as idea—*eidos*), and what the *learning sciences* are really concerned with is selecting methods and techniques that conform to an indelible metaphysical view, *Gestalt*, or world-*as*-picture, that is *productionist* through and through (*metaphysical instrumentalism*). The reader must be aware that a "world picture" is not a mere representation of the world, rather it is the world "conceived and grasped," and hence lived, "as picture" (219), which means that wherever a world picture exists "an essential decision takes place regarding what is, in its entirety" (130). This situation is further made problematic when "methods" (rules, laws, procedures for investigation) are institutionalized, codified, and standardized under the false pretense of representing the rigor and exactitude of science—recall AERA's claims to scientific consistency and rigor in the institutional practice of empirical research in education as introduced earlier.

Based on this reading of Heidegger, it is possible to state that the *learning sciences* already work from a reified, hypostatized view of the human being and thus, for the most part, have *already seen in advance* the results of their research. In the *learning sciences*,

> the "opening up" that occurs in projection of the specific domain of beings does not yet let us understand what such an opening up is as a phenomenon in its historical uniqueness; it does not yet let us understand what is historically distinctive about such an event... In other words, it is a specific way in which discovery is itself understood or "projected" in advance that constitutes the fundamental "opening up" at the basis of modern scientific [educational] research. (McNeill, 1999, 168)

With this in mind, as Heidegger (1977) claims, in the physical sciences, history, and education, "methodology aims at representing what is fixed and stable" (123), at making what it represents into an object in order that those "who calculates can be sure and certain, of that being" and because of this "truth has been transformed into the certainty of representation... the objectiveness of representing" (127). This indicates that there is a very specific metaphysical ground with a view to the human as *subjectum* that underlies modern *science as research*, which gives rise to the "conquest of world as picture" (134). To sum up the view of world-*as*-picture inherent in *science as research*, I review experimentation and explanation in terms that will be related to Froman's (1993) analysis of Renaissance art: (1) *experimentation* in modern science is not about discovery, for the "methodology of modern science, adheres to a rigor that is guaranteed by a fixed 'ground-breaking' schema that is projected in advance of setting up and execution of experimentation," and (2) *explanation* is of what is already known, "provided by the facts that are displayed in the course of experimentation," and the explanation of facts related to the experimentation has "already been brought under the purview of the principles and laws at work in the 'ground-breaking' schema" (Froman, 1993,339). To conclude, as opposed to the "discovery of nature," through experimentation and explanation, modern science "announces the institution and establishment of the already projected 'ground-breaking' schema as nature per se. This identification is inseparable from a mode of world-apprehension whereby world is apprehended as picture," and once this occurs, "the existence of any and every entity is identified with the position that it holds exclusively" (339).

Although Heidegger philosophizes the world-*as*-picture in terms of modernity, Froman's reading primarily focuses on the phenomenon of world-*as*-picture as it manifests in the paintings of the Renaissance, paintings that display "the mode of world-apprehension that is essential to the metaphysical foundations of the modern epoch" (338). Thus, it is possible to classify Renaissance art in Heideggerian terms as "metaphysical art," and this issue of metaphysical art will eventually be related to "action painting" (*abstract expressionism*) as a form of art that is "non-metaphysical" in nature, and hence, holds the potential to inspire us beyond the limited mode of world-*dis-closure* consistent with technology and *science as research*. Analyzing Merleau-Ponty's aesthetics, Froman (1993) argues that Descartes' work on optics (in *Dioptrics*) was informed by the techniques of "perspective" incorporated in Renaissance painting, for not only did the paintings produce a sense of 3-dimensional depth they also, as related to the discussion of world-*as*-picture, provided specific "representations of Being," and so what one sees when looking at a "Renaissance painting is an extracted segment from the world-as-picture, as the segment is seen in two dimensions, on the scale of the canvas" (340). This artistic inspiration available to Descartes, as a late-Renaissance philosopher, extended beyond his work in optics to ultimately play a role in his "working out of the metaphysical foundations of the modern age that entails the apprehension of the world-as-picture" (340). Descartes treats "perspective in geometric terms, as if it were merely a matter of relations in objective space, detached from all human points of view," which indicates that this "account of perspective is not based on attention to the phenomena of lived experience," rather it is grounded in "a priori metaphysical reasoning concerning what matter and perception *must* be like if an objective science is to be possible" (Matthews, 2003, 134).

The Renaissance artist first brings the world to stand within the painting in a systematic manner through the understanding and use of perspective, which in crucial terms, "involves the composition of a fully equilibrated canvas that is first made possible by 'bringing to stand before oneself as standing over and against oneself' of world-as-picture that is self-contained" (Froman, 1993, 340). It is the vanishing point that structures and pre-determines exactly what is painted on the canvas and this "corresponds with the point that is optimal for viewing the painting" (341). What is seen and experienced by the spectator is a world organized around the spectator, in "relation to a subject that takes over the identity of the essential nature of a human being when world is apprehended as picture" (341). It is possible to understand Renaissance art as working within Heidegger's description of how the world-*as*-picture functions in relation to *science-as-research*, experimentation, and explanation. For in the artist's "pictoral" metaphysical *re*-presentation, the

> *re*presentation of anything and everything that appears within the scenes of Renaissance painting, the *re*presentation essential to the apprehension of world-as-picture, is prior to the finished Renaissance painting and is not accomplished by it. The appearance in painting of Renaissance perspective and detail does not mark—any more than does the establishment of modern science with its methodology of experimentation and explanation—a "discovery of nature," but rather announces a mode of world—apprehension whereby world is apprehended as picture. (341)

A view to Renaissance painting emerges in terms of what I have referred to as a "technical" mode of world-*dis-closure*, of "seeing," for technological knowledge displays two key characteristics as related to Renaissance painting: (1) the Renaissance artist comes to the canvas with a preliminary image (*eidos*) in mind, and (2) the artist carries out the activity of painting (*poiesis*) directed toward this preliminary idea/image (*eidos*) with the goal (*telos*) of re-producing it in/as the finished work (*ergon*). Modes of scientific knowing are at once *teleological* and *eidetic*. The product (*ergon*) is grasped before its final actualization in the idea (*eidos*), and the *eidos* directs the activity of making (*poiesis*) in advance, serving as the end-goal (*telos*) of the technical process of manufacturing. The reader will recall that this is precisely the manner in which science-*as*-research functions in relation to the mathematical "object-sphere" in contemporary standardized curriculum and education.

Contributing to Froman's analysis and furthering the theme of Renaissance art as *re*-presenting the world-*as*-picture, as observed by Beardsley (1965), one of the most important components of Renaissance painting is *istoria,* or "the dramatic subject, or scene...the actions, expressed emotions, themes involved in what is going on" (123). To be a good *istoria,* stresses Beardsley, "it must, first, avoid incongruities" (123), and this is crucial to understanding the intimate relationship between Renaissance painting and the literary arts, indeed, painting and sculpture of that historical epoch were "being distinguished from other manual and technical crafts, and earning a place among the 'liberal arts'" (123). Here, the world-*as*-picture is structured by and *re*-presented in terms of Aristotle's ideal definition of Sophoclean tragedy wherein the plot was constructed and "defined primarily in terms of its temporal and logical development" (Puttfarken, 2003, 16). Interestingly, as related to the analysis, as Barrett (1960) observes, the classical plot that was carried over into Renaissance art unfolded "by means of triangle whose apex represents the climax with which everything in the play has some logical and necessary connection" (50). Thus, logic, necessity, rationality, probability, and intelligibility bring a sense of wholeness and coherence, and, indeed, a sense of *teleological* unfolding to the actions and content of the story as depicted. It must be noted, as related to the mechanistic Cartesian world-*as*-picture, this "canon for intelligible literary structure" that brings a coherency to the painted images, "arose in a culture in which the universe too was believed to be an ordered structure, a rational [mechanical] and intelligible whole" (51).

Metaphysical art and non-metaphysical art: the views of Heidegger and Merleau-Ponty

To classify art as "representational" is to classify it with a "theory" of art that falls under the aegis of "realism" or "imitation" in aesthetics. Representational art has the "quality of depiction which allows the viewer to quickly and easily recognize what it is a picture of" and it also has the "quality of a literary text which relates it closely to everyday life" (Sartwel, 1992, 345). There are certain assumptions about representational theory as outlined by Parsons and Blocker (1993) and include: the artwork as transparent medium; the artist does not affect the represented reality; the artwork does not point beyond itself in meaning; art criticism is based on the accuracy of depiction; and the quality of the spectator's aesthetic response is linked to the quality of the depiction (77). Although it is quite correct to link these traits and components with the "representational theory" of art, it is incorrect to link this type of art with what has been referenced as *re*-presentational art, which for Heidegger is "metaphysical art," i.e., art that *re*-presents *metaphysical instrumentalism* within the world-*as*-picture giving a systematic structure to life through the work of art. Although in the previous section I dealt with Descartes, who is the metaphysician par excellence of modernity, *metaphysical instrumentalism* is actually traceable to the "first beginning" of Western philosophy *as* metaphysics, which Heidegger (1998) links with Plato, and, indeed, this makes sense because Descartes was an avowed Platonist.

Art for Heidegger (1993a) is a superlative mode of revelation or *truth-happening*, and this is based on art's authentic "truth function" or the *truth-happening* associated with the "participation" in and "preservation" of the work of art by those who are drawn into art's "work-Being" and experience an *ek-static* mode of attunement. Truth (*aletheia*) as it is revealed in the site of the work is an "event," because it is actually a moment of *aletheuein*, which expresses the entrance or movement into the unfolding of truth as active participant. In the moment of art's attunement, participants *stand-out* (*ek-stasis*) of their everyday modes of existing and are transported into the *lighted clearing* where their historical destiny manifests for potential appropriation (*Ereignis*). Great art, then, is historical founding, a call and evocation of the entrance of a people into their vocation and destiny, and there are for Heidegger two great epochs within which art facilitated a "holy" and renewed relationship with Being and inspired an historical sense of human dwelling: Classical Greece and the Middle Ages. However, as Young (2001) points out, there is "nothing in Western modernity which plays the role played, in Greece, by temple and amphitheatre, and in the Middle Ages, by church and cathedral" (121). Specifically, according to Heidegger (1977), the loss of historical-founding art is due to the *En-framing* effect of technology, for art in the modern era no longer reveals humanity's historical destiny, and, as Heidegger makes clear:

> Enframing does not simply endanger man in his relationship to himself and to everything that is. As a [new] destining, it banishes man into that kind of revealing [*truth- happening*] which is an ordering. Where this ordering holds sway, it drives out every other possibility of revealing. Above all, Enframing conceals that revealing which, in the sense of *poiesis*, lets presence come forth

into appearance. As compared with that other revealing [that of the work of art], the setting-upon that challenges forth thrusts man into a relation to that which is, that is at once antithetical and rigorously ordered. Where Enframing holds sway, regulating and securing of the standing-reserve mark all revealing. (27)

What does it mean to call art "metaphysical," beyond stating that it is art that *re*-presents and thus *re*-produces the world-*as*-picture? First, to call art metaphysical is not the reading or classification (theorizing) of art that reduces it to the realm of beauty, associates it with stirring felicitous emotions, or classifies it in terms of one or another "type" or "theory" of art, e.g., realism, formalism, cognitivism, or post-modernism. Such theorizing is already symptomatic of the loss of art. All the "usual readings and interpretations" of art, according to Heidegger (1996), draw their inspiration "indiscriminately from metaphysics and from the metaphysical doctrine of art, that is, from aesthetics" (18–19). Second, and this is a far more complex issue, to reference art as metaphysical is to focus on its "symbolic" character or nature, "the metaphysical essence of art" has to do with "symbolic images [*ist sinnbildlich*]" (17), whereby image (*Bild*) "stands for what can be perceived sensuously in general," and the symbolic sense (*Sinn*) "is the nonsensuous [*das Nichtsinnliche*], which is understood and given meaning and has been determined in manifold ways in the course of metaphysics" (17–18). The point is that imagery reflects that which can be felt or perceived (the sensuous—*aistheton*) and the symbol refers beyond the perceived imagery to reference the non-sensuous (*noeton*), or the realm of the suprasensuous, e.g., the realm of Plato's *eidoi* or the Christian understanding of Heaven. In short, metaphysical art *re*-presents (world-*as*-picture), through imagery and symbol, a two-world metaphysical schema, with a privilege given over to the suprasensuous realm, i.e., Being over becoming, reality over appearance: "The superior and true are what is sensuously represented in the symbolic image. The essence of art stands and falls in accordance with the essence and truth of metaphysics" (18). Importantly, this indicates that metaphysical art "does not exist just for itself; rather, what is sensuous about the artwork is as it is in the artwork: it exists for the nonsensuous and suprasensuous, for that which is also named the spiritual or spirit," and this indicates the sense of moving from one realm to another, of "going over and beyond," and this is "called *meta* in the Greek" (17).

If this reading were focused exclusively on Heidegger, then it would be necessary to pursue an interpretation of Hölderlin, whose poetry (as essential *Dichtung*) is "non-metaphysical," and by definition, is not "art" at all as conceived by modernity. With the focus on Pinar's (1991) essay, however, the analysis must take a direction that leads away from Hölderlin's poetry to the consideration of a new and potentially radical form of "anti-metaphysical" or non-metaphysical art, namely, the art of abstract expressionism, which I approach through a reading of Merleau-Ponty's (1964, 1974, 1993a) phenomenology of art as it is related to Froman's (1993) analysis of "action-painting." Is it possible that such art might, as a form of non-representational expression of the first-order realm of lived experience or perception, attune us in such a way as to *disclose* a post-metaphysical view of the world? In formulating a rejoinder, it must be understood that in the *age of the world-picture* art is relegated to the "metaphysical" status of mere aesthetic phenomenon, which indicates that art in such a milieu can never be foundational, revelatory, with the power, as Pinar (1991) states, to "allow us to see anew and to understand anew," and "[s]uch is the purpose of high art" (246). As Froman (1993) observes: "In order that art may succeed in providing a possibility of extricating civilization from the extreme danger of our world-historical situation, the relegation of art to the status of the 'merely aesthetic' must be brought to an end" (346), i.e., art must break the hold and sway of technology (*das Ge-stell/En-framing*) in the age of the world-*as*-picture.

Indeed, in the essay, "Eye and Mind," Merleau-Ponty (1993b) argues that due to art's close proximity to our primordial, pre-reflexive lived experience of the world, it is distanced from both the modes of communication and ways of knowing common to both science and philosophy, which he deems "monsters" of Cartesianism. Merleau-Ponty's writings concerned with art, essays spread out over a 16-year period, are attempts to move away from descriptions of the human's Being-in-the-world, as found in such works as *Phenomenology of Perception*, in order to focus on a "post-Cartesian ontology, a non-dualistic study of Being which went beyond (or beneath?) traditional philosophical distinctions and dualisms" (Quinn, 2009, 20). This, I argue, is the search for a "language," a unique form of communication, that lives beyond the metaphysical drive for "manipulation, operationalism, and theoretical models" for conceiving the human being in its world (20). Merleau-Ponty (1993a), in "Cezanne's Doubt," makes the claim that Cezanne's art is unique in that it challenges standard modes of understanding and intellectualizing, Cezanne's art cannot be grasped in terms of rules, principles, or theories of previous aesthetics, and in this it is precisely a work of art that stands outside "metaphysics" and is expressive and meaningful in terms that are new and novel. This is because we encounter in Cezanne a form of art that "is not imitation, nor is it something manufactured according to the wishes of instinct or good taste," rather it is a "process of expression" (67). Cezanne stands outside both the "aesthetic" categorization of "impressionism" and traditional "academic painting." To the point, Cezanne's art stands outside of the way "art had respectively been deemed in the first case by Plato and in the second by Kant and Hume" (Quinn, 2009, 15).

For Merleau-Ponty, art brings together imagination and perception and is akin to phenomenology in terms of what it can reveal. Merleau-Ponty (1969) is interested in the pre-theoretical and pre-conceptual world of pre-reflexive "bodily" activity, because for him, the unmediated "perceived world is always the presupposed foundation of all rationality, all value and all existence" (13). Conceptual and theoretical constructs are presupposed by the pre-reflexive and pre-reflective locomotion of the body as it is immersed in the world, as a "body subject," which is a body that moves and engages the world and others, and which also thinks. Thus, is it not the mind that "thinks," as Nietzsche (1990) always understood, rather it is the body that "thinks" and feels, emotes, moves, and lives. Perception is never mere passive reception on the part of the human subject, who, in terms of Locke's understanding, receives sensate data/input from an objective and external world. Rather, perception is an active and creative act of expression, which brings to life "meanings" that had not hitherto existed. Art is perceptual expression, which manifests through artist's bodily involvement with her world, and this includes her interaction with the canvas, her paints, and the use of her brushes. Art, according to Merleau-Ponty (1993b), is "the expressive operation" that originates in perception, in and through the pre-reflexive convergence and overlapping of the visual field and the field of bodily locomotion, which "amplifies into painting and art" (106–107). The process of "amplification" is the process whereby art is created, and art for Merleau-Ponty is the activity of "translating" and "extending" perception and making it accessible to others, for, much like the *criterion of correctness* in phenomenology, it is through inter-subjectivity that the artist's work accomplishes the *trans*-subjective leap required to make it a viable medium of "truth": The artist as *creator* "must wait for [the painting] to come to life for other people. When it does, the work of art will have united these separate lives; it will no longer exist in one of them like a stubborn dream" (70).

According to Merleau-Ponty, by loosening the hold of second order modes of communication and theoretical constructs, it is possible to put ourselves in touch more deeply with the pre-reflexive world of lived experience, and art (painting) is the superlative medium that makes such a move possible. Art, much like phenomenological description, is a "third way" between empiricist and intellectualist forms of knowing and ordering the world. When writing on Cezanne, Merleau-Ponty claims that the artist's work returns us to the world of pre-reflexive perception at the moment when form is being given to our world. Cezanne's paintings contribute "to the impression of an emerging order, of an object in the act of appearing, organizing itself before our eyes" (65). Participating in Cezanne's paintings facilitates the transcendence beyond instrumental, technical, and scientific modes of cognizing the world. Cezanne discovers and expresses within his paintings that "the lived perspective, that which we actually perceive, is not a geometric or photographic one" (67). The vision he offers "penetrates right to the [ontological] root of things beneath the imposed order of humanity" and "suspends these habits of thought and reveals the base of inhuman nature upon which man [sic] has installed himself" (66). Art provides a more direct medium of access to the lived "body-subject's" pre-reflexive perception than does traditional or technical modes of philosophy, which do so indirectly mediated through a technical and conceptual language. As related to art and language, Besmer (2007) states that what "remains constant throughout Merleau-Ponty's career is the thesis that all linguistic meaning *originates* from perceptual sense," and art allows this realm, in a *poietic* manner, to "show forth" most clearly and dramatically in and through the process of "amplification" (100).

The language we speak, in forms that might be classified as "secondary" modes of expression, "ultimately returns or refers to the perceptual world such that…language is underwritten by perception" (100). However, there always exists the danger that such language will distort the experience it seeks to describe because it employs similar objectifying representations common to scientific description, and the reader will recall that this is a problem already encountered in both Heidegger and Pinar. Painting (art), however, speaks a new and expressive language that reveals features of our lived experience with a sensitivity and concomitant vivacity that outstrip the potential for communication found in instrumental systems of language. As related to my foregoing remarks, according to Froman (1993), painting takes shape and gathers its power to mean and "speak" in terms of a "novel" mode of linguistic expression as mediated by and translated through "the association of traces left on the canvas of an overlap between the field of vision and the field of motor projects. It is this overlap that Merleau-Ponty discovers what he calls 'reversibility'" (344). There is an acute sense of "reversibility" linked to artists, and most particularly, painters, and this

> refers on the one hand to the general ambiguity of the overlapping experienced in a human body to be both perceived [in that it is an object of perception] and perceiver [in that it is also a subject]. On the other hand, it refers to how the painter-seer is intensely caught up and *intertwined* in the midst of the visible, through their affiliation with a medium. By result of their heightened exposure of the visible, the painter may interchange the usual roles of watcher and watched so that they both imagine and physically experience the opposite of what is considered normal. (Quinn, 2009, 22–23)

Regarding this role swapping between human and world, Merleau-Ponty (1993a) recounts Paul Klee's remarks concerning the painting of landscapes, where Klee experienced his role of the observer being reversed, that is to say, there were times when the landscape appeared to be observing him. The human body is ever vacillating between touching and *being* touched, seeing and *being* seen and there is a "gap" that exists at the heart of this pre-reflexive phenomenon. Art, it is possible to say, lives in this invisible, reticent, and pre-reflexive space. The artist or painter has a heightened sense of this pre-reflexive way of Being-in-the-world that for the most part remains unknown to those who are non-artistic. The painter, through the "specially attuned perception attained through his or her relation to an artistic medium, has an aesthetic insight into this 'invisibility,' which means he or she can notice usually hidden 'things'" and is then able to communicate and express this "hidden" view, the ontological essence of "reversibility," through the medium of painting (Quinn, 2009, 23).

As stated, Froman prefers the moniker "action painting" to "abstract expressionism" when describing this movement in mid-twentieth-century art, which includes, in addition to Pollack, de Kooning (*Easter Monday*, 1956), Rothko (*Blue, Orange, Red*, 1961), Hofmann (*Flowering Swamp*, 1957), and Kline (*Meryon*, 1960), to provide an extremely truncated list of the New York School of painters. There is an important reason for this choice of terms, which relates at once to the artist and his participation in the work and also the work itself, which is to say, the way in which the work of art ("action-painting") gathers meaning and opens "worlds," i.e., the work of art's unique form of *truth-happening*. Pollack states the following about the work of art in the modern age and its revelatory power and the uniqueness of its mode of expression: "The modern painter cannot express his age, the airplane, atom bomb, the radio in the old forms of the Renaissance or any other past culture" (as quoted in Brommer, 1988, 471). The role of the artist changes dramatically in this style of art or manifestation of art *as* "event" and this includes the manner in which the canvas is approached and conceived in terms of a flat plane, a vast expanse of potential, a *nothingness* that might read as homage to the well-known existential credo—*existence precedes essence*. Barrett emphasizes these points when stating that in modern "action-painting" there occurs the "*flattening out of all planes* upon the plane of the picture" (Barrett, 1960, 50). No longer is painting understood in terms of the "elements in a configuration that is taking shape," i.e., in the process of arriving at a completed picture as re-presented image, "but rather [becomes] temporary resolutions of strains or tensions in the painter's perceptual field, resolutions that give way to other strains and tensions" (Froman, 1993, 345). Indeed, in "action-painting," the dynamic site of the convergence of body, vision, locomotion, and imagination "becomes the very subject of painting" (344).

"Action-painting" obliterates the *symbol-image* relationship characteristic of metaphysical art described by Heidegger, and it is opposed to Renaissance painting, states Froman, which displays "an extracted segment of a self-contained world apprehended as picture" (347). In addition, action-painting avoids incorporating the literary canon upon which Renaissance painting is dependent. Therefore, action-painting lives beyond symbol, allegory, and metaphor (*metaphora*), and metaphors, as Heidegger (1996) explains, which facilitate transference, "likewise belong to symbols and images" in that "symbolic images in the broadest sense," which can be "sensuously intuited, exemplifies and furnishes us with a rule that cannot be grasped sensuously" (16). Beyond Renaissance painting, Froman (1993) separates action-painting from the tradition of art history by noting two important and radical characteristics of the movement, which were introduced above: (1) it departs from the tradition of "rendering a prior image on the canvas" and (2) it departs from the "procedures working toward the aim of engendering an image on the canvas," and due to these approaches to art "action painting more radically discomposes the world-as-picture displayed by premodern painting than does the work by Klee or by other progeny of Klee" (345). Artist, art, and site converge in an "event" of *truth-happening* when "the artist comes to the canvas as a site for acting," and the "painting displays the event that takes place when the artist paints, rather than conceals this event in favor of an equilibrated composition that displays an extracted segment of a self-contained world apprehended as picture" (343).

Action-painting acquires its power *as* art to gather meaning in the tension between artist and painting, which, "by way of traces of the overlap between the visual and motor fields," a transformation occurs, and this is the re-attunement that overturns *metaphysical instrumentalism*, for "the effect is to discompose the apprehension of the painting as itself, a region of a world apprehended as picture" (346). It is through the unique, or "expressive," language of painting, that Merleau-Ponty (1969) claims that we are shown something radically new, through which we glean a new form of understanding from our experience of art. In the presence of the canvas as the site of convergence of the "lived body," we "perceive in a total way with [our] whole being: [we] grasp a unique structure of the thing, a unique way of being, which speaks to all [our] senses at once" (50). The art of "action-painting" exists in terms of nothing other than itself, and functions, according to Froman (1993), as an "origin" (*Ursprungen*), for it reveals the "dynamic in which the art of painting originates," it establishes the "motion of painting" *as* the "subject of painting," and in doing so, breaks open an open space wherein all that is seen and experienced, all that is brought to *presence* for appropriation, is new, and this is possible because action-painting heralds the "end to the fixed boundaries of art that has been relegated to the status of the merely aesthetic'" (347).

To conclude this analysis, action-painting is a form of art in the modern age that inspires our re-attunement through which the grip of technology is loosened, for it resists the act of *re*-presenting the world-*as*-picture that is crucial to the perpetuation and re-production of *metaphysical instrumentalism*. In light of this claim, action-painting is a form of legitimate art that lives as the harbinger of the overcoming of metaphysics, challenging all forms of systematic and calculative forms of thought in and through its sheer immeasurability as art. Moving to the final section, focused on Pinar's (1991) original thoughts that began the chapter, I remind the reader that the purpose of "abstract expressionist" scholarship is to write "the maelstrom of experience" (248) as it draws its life-blood from the origin and "revelatory function of art," and much like "abstract expressionism" (action-painting), this form of scholarship "takes flight and widens the eye, and reveals anew the world which comes to form through our imagination, our labor, and lives" (249). The emergence of new forms of phenomenological scholarship in education and curriculum might be related to the advent or eruption of "action-painting" unto the modern scene, and this is traceable to both art's authentic "truth function," or the *truth-happening*, in conjunction with a mode of attunement that reconfigures our powers of interpretation and understanding, which is associated with and engendered by the work of art. I now move to develop the notion of a "painterly" and "poietic" language that emerges from the understanding of both Heidegger and Merleau-Ponty as related to the reading, writing, and "saying" of curriculum in Pinar's "abstract expressionist" scholarship.

Abstract expressionist scholarship: the poeitic and painterly "saying" of curriculum beyond metaphysical instrumentalism

To embrace "abstract expressionist" scholarship "is to attempt [an order] of writing, writing that aspires to, and at times, exemplifies, the revelatory function of art" (Pinar, 1991, 249). This I suggest might be understood in terms of Merleau-Ponty's notion of a "painterly" form of expressive communication that lives beyond the instrumental function of language and the *natural attitude* and demonstrates a resonance with Heidegger's meditative elucidation of language as a "poietic" phenomenon. "Abstract expressionist" scholarship in curriculum studies manifests in the dual concern for the avoidance of "dogmatism" in curriculum research as well as the crucial turn from the presentation of research findings in terms of representational, and hence objectified and reified, results or conclusions in terms of generalizations. Both of these concerns require a move beyond the attunement of technology and *metaphysical instrumentalism*, which, according to Pinar, might draw its inspiration from the art of abstract expressionism (action-painting). As stated, the world-*as*-picture is not simply a conceptual structure organizing our ideas about the world, rather it is mode of world disclosure that in great part determines the manner in which entities and world show up for our appropriation, giving the overall frame-work or structure of our *Being-in-the-world*—i.e., *we live out the world-as-picture*. In curriculum studies, we might link this phenomenon with what Daignault (1992) terms the "simulacra" of curriculum, which exercise a powerful control over all aspects of our lives, determining everything down to the manner in which our Being unfolds, e.g., they determine our "sensible" and "perceptible" experience of time, yet are themselves "not sensible" (205). However, the "images" produced are "entirely perceptible; they are images of objects composed by the fall of atoms" (205). They work, for the most part, in a stealth and undetected way to inspire a "false sense of sentiment of will and desire in sensibilities. They produce the mirage of a false infinity in the images they form" (205). Simulacra take on the life of what we might link to true "reality" over that of mere "appearance," assuming a sense of "permanence" over "change," when in fact they are vaporous, illusory productions of the technological attunement of the age. Perhaps the most blatant and obvious instance of simulacra at work in curriculum is traceable to the categories of standardization in all of its virulent forms.

From his earliest writings onward, Pinar has sought to understand curriculum without *re*-presenting it, and thus reifying and objectifying it, in language, e.g., in his understanding of curriculum in and through the Latin infinitive *currere*. To *poietize* and preserve the mystery of curriculum without destroying the sublimity of its potential to gather and reveal meanings in a multiplicity of ways, appears paradoxical, and above all, nebulous and obtuse, but this need not be the case. Gelven (1972) explains how language might be conceived in a non-objectifying manner within the *inquiry* or quest for "self-knowledge," when seeking to "further deepen one's [personal] understanding" (7). Gelven informs us that questioning into the nature of our Being carried out in the grammatical mode of the "infinitival" provides the "linguistic structure necessary" for *self-inquiry* wherein that which is thought most authentically is irreducible to a "mere logical subject or object" (80)! Gelven goes on to explain the crucial role that the mode of the infinitive plays in forms of *self-inquiry*, and he begins by dispelling a common and erroneous view of infinitives: "To define infinitives as verbal nouns is a mistake. To be sure, infinitives can be used grammatically as subjects and objects of sentences, but this does not make them into nouns, for nouns refer to things and objects" (81). Importantly, it is possible to grasp the crucial aspect of "motion," i.e., the movement of life itself, which draws us and holds us in the context or sway of the inquiry. Bound up with the signification of the mode of the infinitival is that it is "verbal" in its essence. For an "infinitive is *verbal* in that it signifies being or doing" (80), and it is linked with tracing and illuminating the "how" of the unfolding of that which is of concern, and we must keep in mind that the infinitive "is a noun only in the sense that it can be talked about, not that it is substantized in any metaphysical sense" (80). As Gelven makes clear, *"The purpose of the infinitive is to provide language with the ability to talk about modes of existence without reference to a particular subject and without objectifying or substantizing what is talked about"* (80).

As stated, this crucial understanding of the language of infinitives relating to the expression of *self-inquiry* in *currere* is grammatical in nature. Here, language does succeed in manifesting a *showing* that heralds and welcomes "something as abiding into the range of its expressibility" (69). However, it must be noted that grammatical categories and rules for combining words or lexical categories, e.g., that nouns have distributional and inflectional properties, do not touch on the ontology of language and still live at the "theoretical" level. To take the analysis beyond the discussion of the grammatical mode of the infinitival, it is possible to understand language in its *ontological* function to gather and grant meaning and impart traces of linguistic signification in new ways as related to the foregoing analysis of art. For the artistic image, according to Matthews (2003), "having its own, non-conventional, meaning, is able to give 'knowledge of truth' in a sense that seems to be something more like a *fresh* or *unconventional understanding* of the event depicted," or as in the case of "action-painting," of the merging and spontaneous interplay of lines, colors, and shapes on the canvas. As Pinar (1991) claims, to read and write *curriculum as an abstract expressionist phenomenon* requires a form of communication, which is "more intellectually experimental and revelatory than 'representational' scholarship permits" (247), which might allow researchers to read and write the "portrait" of curriculum in a non-representational manner, and this calls for an "aesthetic" approach. This I suggest might be related to the "poietic" in Heidegger and the "painterly" in Merleau-Ponty, wherein rather than *seeing the ends of education in advance,* researchers are attuned to *listening in advance* for the call of education that is on the approach from out of and is immanent within the essential unfolding of the "lived" curriculum (*curriculum vitae*) in moments of learning when the ontological address of education "speaks" from out of the primordial depths of its reticence. Indeed, for Heidegger (2001), language originates in "silence" and the "[b]earing of silence arises out of the essentially occurring origin of language itself" (65/78). Similarly, in Merleau-Ponty's (1993c) philosophy, it is the "expressive" language of painting that speaks most originally and uniquely from out of "the source of silent and solitary experience on which culture and the exchange of ideas have been built in order to take cognizance of it" (69).

As stated in the introduction, I retain the original Attic Greek form of the English word "poetic," which is *poietic* as related to *poiesis*. Heidegger incorporates the term in its relation to *physis*, or "the unfolding of nature." Vallega-Neu (2013) states that "poiesis" for Heidegger always refers to an *originary* process of "bringing forth" what comes to *presence*. Language that is by nature *poietic* facilitates and shelters "the 'bringing forth' of (and not simply 'speaking about') being as a historical event" (140). The poietic language that might be associated with Pinar's notion of "abstract expressionist" scholarship is *affective* in nature and brings to light the crucial "difference between propositional language (*Aussage*) and saying (*Sage*) (i.e., original [*ursprunglich*] or inceptive [*anfanglich*] language" (Vallega-Neu, 2001, 67). Language in this view is not a "possession" or creation of the human being; rather it is a gift or bestowal, it is an "inceptive response to [Being's] call that first opens this call by echoing it in words" (69), i.e., we are moved by the address of the world and are drawn out of the "silence," for *poietizing* phenomena does not begin or originate with "speech but rather with speechlessness in the lack of the word of [Being] that points to the silent abysmal source of [Being]" (72). Poietic language preserves and shelters the *primal mystery*, or the ontological aspects of our being-in-the-world, allowing it to be *as* mystery. For in "contrast to words uttered in propositional speech, where any trace of the occurrence of being [the *primal mystery*] as enownment" (the possibility of appropriating that which is most our own)—in relation to human *transcendence* and the *presencing* that first grants access to our possibilities for appropriation and comportment—"is covered up," while "poietic words are able to shelter the withdrawal of [Being] by echoing it" (75).

Heidegger (1962) makes the distinction between the "apophantic" use of "as" and the more original use of "as" in hermeneutic interpretation, and the "primordial 'as' of an interpretation (*hermeneia*) which understands circumspectively we call the existential-*hermeneutical* 'as' in distinction from the *apophantical* 'as' of the assertion" (201/158). In *Being and Time*, where Heidegger introduced the phenomenological-hermeneutic as *fundamental ontology* of Dasein privileged this so-called "hermeneutic *as* of interpretation" (the hermeneutics of Dasein's facticity) was privileged in terms of providing primordial access to Dasien's way of Being-in-the-world. However, as Heidegger moves into the 1930s a different view of language emerges in his work (McNeill, 2006; Dahlstrom, 2013; Polt, 2013; Vallega-Neu, 2013). This language, as McNeill (2006) points out is grounded in an "originary *poiesis*," more primordial than the language of hermeneutics, which is attuned to being's arrival, to the "coming to pass of a world" (138). This language

> would presumably not yet be a discourse seeking to determine something "as" something—not a *legein ti kata tinos*—whether that of the apophantic discourse of science, the apophantic-hermeneutic discourse of Heidegger's early phenomenology, or indeed that of the hermeneutic deliberation of Aristotelian *phronesis*, all of which are dianoetic ["through cognition"], and concerned with determining that which already manifests itself in a certain way. (138–139)

In the realm of standardized education and its research, there is the predisposition toward *dianoetic* language as described by McNeill with the concomitant leaning to understand language primarily in terms of an oral phenomenon and neglect or forget that it is, in its essential ontological unfolding, an "aural" phenomenon, which requires a "listening" for in order to assume a stance within the primordial silence that first gives language. The *poietic* saying as an intimate expression of Being, as a gesturing and intimating, is the "saying that bears silence," and in this conception of language, "its word is not by any other means merely a sign for something quite other. What it names is what is meant" (Heidegger, 2001, 65/78).

Heidegger's view of *poietic* language that emerges from silence to *thinking and questioning* might be related to the ongoing and ever renewed process of learning in an original manner. Vallega-Neu (2001) brings attention to the crucial issue of renewing thought through the careful attention to language, for "[t]hinking needs always to leap anew into a realm of thinking that has not been explored or said in this way before" (77). Indeed, this is precisely how Pinar (1991) envisions the "saying" of curriculum inspired by "abstract expressionism," which is not located in the drive to "prove a point, not to inculcate a dogma, not to create techniques that will work anywhere, anytime, with anybody," rather curriculum theorizing is the "search for vision, for revelation that is original, unique, and that opens the knowing and appreciative eye to worlds hitherto unseen and unknown" (246). The "search for vision," however, is never a destination at which we arrive, in terms of a goal, objective, or aim that is realized or actualized through the process of inquiry. Rather, it is a thinking, questioning, and "saying" that harbors the primordial "danger" inherent to language itself, namely, the potential of "poietic" saying to recede into oblivion, and for this reason, as Vallega-Neu (2001) warns, the "leap has always to be enacted anew because language tends to slip back into its metaphysical character, words tend to transform into mere words that make up propositions about given objects" (77).

Young (2001) contributes to these thoughts when stating that representational thinking and writing, in its attempt to "capture, to represent, to conceptually picture 'the mystery,'" by turning it into an "object" or "entity," thereby blasphemes and obliterates the *mystery* (139). Non-metaphysical art, or "anti-metaphysical art," according to Young, and the form of communication that is consistent with it, allows the *mystery* to show itself in its own self-showing, and here, mystery is expressive of the primordial and ontological "silence" and "reticence" that grounds language. Poietic language affords the potential to momentarily bring the world to stand in the original gathering power of language, "*without* turning it into a highest member of the world...*without* falling into the self-defeating trap of turning it into another occult being" (140). This idea clearly shares ties with Pinar's notion that art, as well as the type of scholarship (*Study Not Curriculum/Teaching Not Testing*) transcending the *metaphysical instrumentalism*, will attend to the silence, reticence, the caesura at the heart of all authentic conversation and

> will be a thematizing that is not representing. For as soon as "representational thinking" [language] comes into play—thinking that is limited to and confined within a horizon that articulates reality into an intelligible world of beings—that which is thematized [*as* objectified] becomes "reified" into a being. (140)

The "painterly" language that might be drawn from Merleau-Ponty's (1993c) philosophy, much like "poietic saying," is a form of language that highlights the difference between an authentic and expressive saying, which formulates things anew, for the first time, and second-order linguistic expressions, i.e., "speech about speech, which makes up the general run of empirical language" (207). The latter form of expression and language, which is always an occurrence of "translation" from original perceptions to the realm of meaningful expressions, is the "operation through which a certain arrangement of already available signs and significations [second-order expression] alters and there transfigures each one of them, so that in the end signification is secreted" (207).

Because it draws on already available signs and significations, secondary expressions articulate the world in ways that are familiar to us, while primary expressions, or "novel expressions," say and show us something new, different, and unique about the world. For Merleau-Ponty, this is precisely the type of "expressive" language that changes, transforms, and ultimately attunes us in an *ek-static* manner, facilitating our "standing-outside" of "second-order" modes of world-*dis*-closure, engendering our transcendence beyond modes of instrumental thought and language. He links primary/expressive language with poets, authors, and most importantly, painters such as Cezanne. The multiplicity of rich, dense, and complex meanings that painting evokes makes its form of communication unique, which is always highlighted by the "silence" that lies at the essence of its language, for there are always aspects of art's meaning that recedes into *mystery*, that remain concealed because they are recalcitrant to formalist and theoretical analyses of "aesthetics". As introduced earlier, Quinn (2009) reminds us that for Merleau-Ponty, "painting gives expression to the 'silent' domain of pre-reflexive bodily relationships and engagements" (19), and it is in and through our participation in action-painting, that the pre-reflexive and pre-reflective field of bodily action and field of vision manifest and are communicated in and through the traces left on the canvas by means of the artist's involvement in the act of painting, the original locus of the "body-subject's" engagement with the world of art.

For Merleau-Ponty, as it is for Heidegger, and this relates directly to Pinar's concern with the authentic reading and writing of curriculum, the authentic language that brings the world to *presence* is a language that speaks "of" phenomena as opposed to speaking "about" them. Second-order discourse cannot capture the many and varied meanings emerging from our participation in the work of art. This is because the "medium of the resulting work is not conventionally referring language, whatever meaning it has will not be expressible in any other terms than those of the work itself" (Matthews, 2003, 139). However, this does not indicate that its meaning is either arbitrary or insignificant, because although as participants and interpreters we cannot provide a single or correct interpretation, "it does not follow that we can give the work any meaning we care to" (139). This indicates that art requires that we say something new and unique as related to its address, its call. The reason that the language of art, most specifically the painter, holds the power to say something radically new and different, is that unlike the literary artist, who "creates new significations for the expressions of his inherited language," the painter is unique in that she creates "language anew" (158). This is a crucial aspect of understanding the form of language that will be required to speak curriculum in terms of "abstract expressionist" scholarship, for as related to painting, new concepts will be necessary and a new way of writing and speaking of curriculum will be required. "Novel expression," writes Besmer (2007), for example, the language associated with the art of painting, "which feeds off, but which also, in the end, surpasses, established truths does not merely tell but *shows* the things themselves" (86). If curriculum studies and theorizing are to break free of technology's attunement (*das Ge-stell*), or *metaphysical of instrumentalism*, then a new language is required, one that is born of art and one that holds the potential to facilitate the speaker, the researcher, in saying something new, and such a language

> exploits the hitherto undetermined possibilities inherent in spoken language in a linguistic event in which the speaking subject surpasses the conventions and the established relationships in language toward the things themselves...Novel expression, thus leaves an "echo." For every expression is, in itself, incomplete. It is an incompleteness that calls for a sequel, which seeks to bring to full expression all that was implied in the silence and latency of the already said. (87–88)

"Abstract expressionist" scholarship embraces the fluid, malleable, and unpredictable nature of human existence as an ever-renewed phenomenon of becoming *other* in the persistent face of the *other*, and this becoming *other* indeed unfolds in terms of an original form of "learning," in term of our *lived curriculum* or *curriculum vitae*. Much like action-painting, "abstract expressionist" scholarship is open to the address of the many and varied phenomena of education. For example, when reading and writing *curriculum* as "abstract expressionist" scholarship, we are no longer seeing and experiencing "this present time," in terms of a persistent present or *presence*, i.e., metaphysical time and presence. Rather, we are transported in an *ek-static* mode of attunement, whereby we "stand-out" to a new "time" where the past comes to meet us from out of the indeterminate future. Life, as it presents itself, or better, comes to *presence* for our potential appropriation, is revealed in a transfigured manner, as experienced in Pollack's abstractions, in terms of wild and unpredictable textured lines of color running through the plane of the canvas, crashing and colliding, breaking off and swirling with a seemingly uncontrolled force of motion, a maelstrom of pre-reflexive "bodily" activity as engaged Being-in-the-world, seemingly without a discernable beginning or end. For Pinar (1991), writing that communicates without re-presentation and preserves the sense of the deep, silent *mystery* in all things, might be understood as relating to the "poietic" language of Heidegger and the "painterly" language of Merleau-Ponty. Such curriculum writing *poietizes* and *paints* life's moments of "immediacy and dissociation, absence and presence, the simultaneity of complexity and simplicity, not just life against death, but life *and* death, including death in life" (248).

I have attempted to reveal "abstract expressionist" scholarship in its irreducible and intimate relationship to language, which requires a re-conceived understanding of language, a form or novel or expressive language that draws its *originary* power and inspiration from art (paining). Such a language that it both *poietic* and *painterly* would "bring forth" hitherto unseen or occluded aspects of the phenomenon of learning, letting these "hidden" aspects show themselves in a new light, in ways that allow curriculum to be the concern of our inquiries while sheltering and preserving those aspects that are recalcitrant to our inquiries and questions. Such language would, as it gathers its power as a medium of *truth-happening*, facilitating that which comes to *presence* to do so in a way that it shines and scintillates with a new light, where the phenomenon's question-worthy aspects might inspire our continued thinking that develops along new lines, follows newly revealed pathways, which would have otherwise remained concealed had not our curriculum practices been inspired by the work of art. Such language, like the brush of the "action-painter," leaves traces of the "lived world" of the curriculum, and through dramatic and bold, and, at times, subtle gestures, *poietically* and in a *painterly* manner, "translates" our experience and communicates this re-conceived and ever-evolving understanding to others. Such a language works similarly to art as a superlative mode of *dis-closure* or *truth-happening*, i.e., it is a medium for the "translation" of phenomena, which resist the calculative and quantitative modes of "standardized" usage in curriculum's instrumental language, in a way that carries *traces* of our original ontological ways of Being-in-the-world. McNeill's (2006) thoughtful reminder will do well to bring these thoughts to a close. For in relation to Pinar's urging that new concepts are necessary for *another inception* of reconceptualist curriculum theorizing, McNeill observes that whenever there is a concern for new concepts, new ways of approaching the issues of our concern, and new beginnings, "translation will be the issue facing us" (116), and it is left to curriculum researchers, professionals, and theorists to decide, at this crucial juncture in the history of education, whether they will confront it or evade it.

3
The Phenomenology of Nature and the *Ēthos* (ηθοζ) of Earthly Dwelling in Jardine and Bonnett: Ecopedagogy, Transcendence, and the Post-Humanist Integrated Curriculum-of-life (*Curriculum Vitae*)

Magrini, James. M. New Approaches to Curriculum as Phenomenological Text: Continental Philosophy and Ontological Inquiry. New York: Palgrave Macmillan, 2015. DOI: 10.1057/9781137573186.0005.

In this final chapter I move in a different, but related, direction to further the contemporary discussion concerning the fate of the earth as it is bound inextricably with the future of curriculum and education by analyzing the phenomenological ontology of curriculum theorist David Jardine and philosopher of education Michael Bonnett. Both thinkers have contributed monumentally to the philosophy of what I cautiously term the *phenomenological-ontology of deep ecology*, or, as Thomson (2009) refers to it, "eco-phenomenology" (445). I am concerned with understanding and drawing out for the reader the intimate, primordial relationship between the human being and nature/Earth, which is already a deep pedagogical phenomenon wherein learning and teaching arise and transpire by means of the ever-evolving "conversation" that humans have and *have always had* with nature as "self-arising" phenomenon. Our "conversation," or intimate primordial relationship with nature/Earth, has been occluded by the attunement of *metaphysical instrumentalism,* and so the chapter deals with the potential "recovery" of, in a most *originary* manner, the forgotten ontological ties to nature. I present the analysis and interpretation, which integrates the Continental philosophy of both Martin Heidegger and Gabriel Marcel, in four sections: (1) I introduce the notions of the de-centered phenomenological subject through the lens of "post-humanism," which foregrounds the potential re-awakening to an ontological awareness of nature and the transcendent; (2) I present Jardine's crucial notion of "eco-pedagogy" in its relation to a view to education that demonstrates a respect for the Earth and the unfolding of what Jardine calls the "integrated curriculum of life" (*Curriculum Vitae*); (3) I focus on Bonnett's analysis of nature as a "self arising" and value-laden phenomenon, which instantiates an integrity and nobility that instill in us a sense of awe, respect, and beholden-ness, which grounds and guides our response to nature's *originary* overarching address, communicated in the reticence of its sway and unfolding, within which we are integral participants; and (4) I conclude with a poetic discussion of *originary* in-dwelling that brings together both Bonnett and Jardine, focused on "emplaced transcendence," which attunes us to the lessons that nature might teach, as evidenced in the intimate conversations to be had on a dense forest path with woodland creatures.

The post-humanist view of the de-centered phenomenological subject in its ontological relation to nature/earth

Throughout this book I have been critical of *metaphysical instrumentalism*, which Bonnett (2015b) calls the "metaphysics of mastery." In this view reason is privileged as the superior human capacity with which to "know" the world. Nature is understood in terms of a causal-mechanistic "machine"—nature is the *objective* and *external other*—which reinforces the catastrophic drive (the technical *will to power*) to master and subjugate nature in an *instrumental* manner, harnessing it for human purposes. Some of these concerns have already been dealt with in my discussion of Cartesian dualism. However, the issue of "privileging of human reason" requires a bit of unpacking for the reader because this view is properly linked, not to Descartes, because for Descartes, it is God who ultimately *brings the world,* but rather to Kant's philosophy in the *Critique of Pure Reason*. I explain this position in some detail, for in addition to representing one of the driving ideas behind *metaphysical instrumentalism,* as related to education and *analytic-empirical* modes of curriculum research and curriculum theory, Kant's philosophy is the breaking point marking the schism dividing Analytic and Continental philosophical thought. Critchley (2001) informs us that this division occurs depending on how one is reading Kant, e.g., is the reading limited to Kant's First critique or the *Critique of Pure Reason* or is it inspired "by the greater systematic ambitions of the Third Critique or *Critique of the Power of Judgment*" (17)? On Critchley's account, the first reading is focused primarily on epistemology and the transcendental subject's relation to the world in and through knowledge, concerning whether or not Kant "successfully provides a valid foundation or grounding for empirical knowledge that meets the challenge of the skepticism of David Hume" (17). Here, Kant is understood as making a contribution to the philosophy of science, and indeed this is how Kant is read by the analytics, or Anglo-American philosophers. However, if Kant is read in light of the Third critique, "then the burning issue of Kant's philosophy becomes the plausibility of the relation between pure and practical reason, nature and freedom, or the unity of theory and practice," and these issues are linked to ethics, aesthetics, and human autonomy. This is "precisely the route followed by the German idealists," e.g., Fichte, Schelling, and Hegel, and it is "arguably the route that Continental philosophy has followed ever since" (19).

Enlisting Jardine (1998), it is now to a brief analysis of Kant that I turn to demonstrate how Kant's First Critique sets up the relationship between the human and the natural world in terms of *epistemological directionality* where the objective world conforms to human concepts and not the reverse. Thus, the movement of our understanding is represented in "subjectivist" terms (human ⇒ world ⇒ *meaning*). In Kant, systematic *a priori* judgments are possible by means of pure intuitions, which are linked with *a priori synthetic judgments,* e.g., time, space, and causality are not somehow "out there" in the world, rather they are in the mind in terms of "categories of the mind," or understanding, and they provide structure and form to our perceptions received from the external world. Since all humans posses these so-called "categories of the mind," this gives rise to Kant's notion of the *transcendental subject,* and further, since the mind produces ideas of the external world, and the mind and its ideas give form to that world, Kant's philosophy, a bridging of the gap between rationalism and empiricism, is classified as *transcendental idealism.* Kant (1956) states this position, regarding the *epistemological directionality* of knowledge in relation to the world, in the following passage:

> Hitherto it has been assumed that all our knowledge must conform to objects. But all attempts to extend our knowledge of objects by establishing something in regard to them a priori, by means of concepts, have, on this assumption, ended in failure. We must therefore make trial whether we may not have more success in tasks of metaphysics, if we suppose that objects must conform to our knowledge. (22)

Whereas Copernicus places the sun at the center of the universe by de-centering and displacing the Earth, Kant establishes human reason as the "center of the *knowable* Universe," and reason determines the possibility of knowledge. Reason, as a "synthesizing faculty, bestows order upon the universe, turning the chaotic influx of experience into a knowable (i.e., orderly) *cosmos*" —reason in this sense is "*constructive of a world*" (Jardine, 1998, 106). This exacts a catastrophic influence on the way the human being experiences the natural world, for Kant's philosophy gives us a view of the subject "who is severed and separate from the Earth" (107), and this subject is no longer "housed" by the Earth, but rather stands against it as subject before an object. According to Jardine, Kant "embodies the denial that the Earth somehow guides us, sustains us, and bears us up" (107), and makes "us and our children *of* the Earth"—in Kant, as Jardine solemnly observes, "ecological disaster is already foretold" (108). For in and through the Kantian legacy "the spirit of the Earth, its inner fire, its *logos*, becomes ourselves. Eco-logos has become ego-logo" (112). Bound up with this analysis is the crucial issue of *epistemological directionality*, which will be addressed below as I bring Heidegger into the discussion. The reader will be asked to keep in mind what Jardine indicates about Kant as it relates to the forthcoming critique of metaphysical humanism and anthropocentricism. In and through Kant,

> we become the ones to whom the Earth must present itself. Reason creates and controls and delimits the "space" within which things are brought into their own and flourish. Things come into their own only within the orbit of human dominion... the earth is there for *us*... since the Earth gains integrity from us, we can colonize it without hesitation, for this simply fulfills what it already prescribed *a priori*. (112)

Both Jardine (1998, 2001) and Bonnett (2004, 2015b) are highly critical of the form of humanism derided by Gray (2003, 2004, 2007), which is the spawn of religious eschatology that has been secularized within the *neo-liberal* view to unadulterated human progress: "Humanism can mean many things, but for us it means belief in progress. To believe in progress is to believe that, by using the new powers given us by growing scientific knowledge, humans can free themselves from the limits that frame the lives of other animals" (4). However, neither Jardine nor Bonnett fall victim to the snares and pitfalls lurking in Gray's philosophy as observed by Critchley (2010), who labels it "passive nihilism," in that Gray "looks at the world from a certain highly cultivated detachment and finds it meaningless," and rather than inspiring ecumenical prescriptive action, which would be a pointless endeavor, he "withdraws to a safe distance and cultivates [an] aesthetic sensibility" (37). Jardine and Bonnett believe the potential for a renewed and revitalized relationship with nature/Earth and education is possible in terms of a "post-humanist" view that affords the attuned perspective to "experience nature," as related to curriculum and education, "as a transcendent other that warrants respect and possesses inherent intrinsic value" (Bonnett, 2013, 194). What does Bonnett mean by "post-humanism" as it is differentiated from *metaphysical* (secular) humanism? Heidegger (1993b) informs us that every form of humanism "is either grounded in a metaphysics or is itself made to be the ground of one," for humanism shares a quality inherent in all metaphysical thought, namely, the way that "the essence of man is determined," and this determination presupposes a concern with and interpretation of "beings without asking about the truth of being," and for this reason, to reiterate, "every humanism remains metaphysical" (225–226).

The term "post-humanism" in Bonnett must not be equated with the rise of machines, robots, and cyborgs to such a degree that the "human" or "humane" elements of existence are transformed or occluded. Rather, Bonnett (2004) views post-humanism as "advocating a certain recognition of the authority of nature," which as opposed to the sense of servitude found in medieval and Renaissance views, "recognizes that human beings have accumulated profound power, choices and responsibilities" (168). On this point, Bonnett is careful to mention that while not denying the human's autonomy, it "acknowledges its limits and recommends that we refrain from using it in ways essentially destructive to ourselves and nature" (168). Bonnett (2004, 2015b) approaches secular humanism with a similar view to its grounding in metaphysics as that of Heidegger, and Bonnett identifies three key characteristics of this view to anthropocentric voluntarism, and these components emerge directly from the analysis of both Descartes and Kant: (1) "the elevation of human reason as the means to understanding the world [is] linked to reinforcing aspirations and belief in the possibilities of subjugating nature to the service of human purposes"; and (2) "the supposition that nature is to be adequately accounted in terms of humanly constructed categories, and that it is susceptible of interrogation and explanation in terms of humanly constructed theories"; and (3) "the most fundamental structures of nature are taken to be purely physical matter/energy operating according to [discernable] universal laws: a mechanical causal or probabilistic system possessing/generating no internal significances and therefore incapable of possessing inherent intrinsic value" (Heidegger, 1993b, 1–2).

The secular humanism that Jardine, Bonnett, and Heidegger (1993b) are critical of exhibits a "self-assertive sense of an entitlement to master nature and bring it into the service of self-given human purposes and desires" (Jardine, 2000, 152). The primary mode of mastery comes via the "transformation of nature as underlying reality through that movement towards the mathematisation of science," which "comes to understand nature itself as governed by the laws of mathematics," and, as related to the discussion of Heidegger's world-*as*-picture (chapter 2), for such a "redolent science to describe and explain things, increasingly it has to set them up as explainable in advance—as instances of pre-defined categories—and in doing so it annihilates the particularity of the individual thing" (153). If nature is perceived in terms of an explainable and hence controllable phenomenon, then there "need be no mysterious remainder in a system of uniform objects whose motions are governed by external forces that are mathematically describable" (153). In humanism there is a perfectionist drive for human progress that demonstrates a "metaphysical *dissatisfaction* that infects our relationship with nature. The world is not good enough as it is; we need *progress*—humanity organized and increasingly modulated through mathematization" (155). The pernicious and impoverished view of nature or the Earth that emerges from secular humanism instantiates a view toward "scientism," which Bonnett (2015b) defines as the view where "experimental scientific thinking has a privileged access to the nature of reality; that somehow its methods, findings and constructions reveal what is 'really' real and that therefore it can assume the mantle of arbiter for thinking in general" (3). In this view, the human subject is the potential master of nature through the exercise of the technical and scientific *will to power*, and this view of the subject in secular humanism must be reconceived and transformed in terms of an authentic *phenomenological subject* who is radically de-centered in the presence of Nature (as "self-arising")/Earth if the transformation and overcoming of the "metaphysics of mastery" is to occur.

There is a substantial notion of the subject, or *phenomenological subject*, in both Jardine (2000) and Bonnett (2013). For example, Bonnett describes the subject in the following terms: The subject has a life of its own, an *identity*, which might be described in terms of a "subject-in-transition," or a subject in the *process-of-becoming other*, and although it is shaped by its historical contextual influences, it is not "some sort of concrescence" of those influences— "it has an internal unity of its own and therefore a perspective on the world that is unique; it has feelings and a basic apprehension of its own existence—its experiences have the quality of 'mineness' and of privacy; it is finite, having only one life to live and this life is the some of all that is possible for that individual" (42–43). From the perspective of "critical theory," or *critical pedagogy* in curriculum studies, it is possible to interpret these "contextual influences" at work on the individual in terms of disciplines and the various webs of power/knowledge structures at work in the social, political, and economic arenas. However, in line with the themes of this text, our attention must be turned toward "contextual influences" that importantly include our interaction and *ecological* relationship with nature/Earth, and what this calls for is not a redefinition of the subject as eloquently described by

Bonnett, but rather an understanding of how that very *phenomenological subject* must be radically de-centered in light of the unique relationship to nature I present in the forthcoming sections.

The shift in the radical de-centering of the subject in relation to Nature/Earth indicates not only a change in *directionality* concerned with *meaning*, from human ⇒ world ⇒ *meaning to* meaning's source (*Nature-Earth*) ⇒ human (as integral participant in *Source*), it also announces a change in *philosophical focus*, which is now understood as a concern for what is most *primordial* in human existence, and this is the crucial phenomenological shift from epistemological concerns to ontological concerns. Thus, this shift is not the mere alteration of our "mind-set" or our theoretical orientation, a change in the "conceptual lens," as it were, through which we view the issue of human meaning. Rather, as argued throughout the book, it is a radical change in attunement, which indicates that when a stance is taken in relation to our understating of nature, of the Earth, our pedagogical responsibilities hang in the balance. The attunement of which both Jardine (2000) and Bonnett (2013, 2015b) speak of is a re-awakening to the transcendent power and *mystery of* nature, its radical alterity, and its value-laden essence. In Bonnett (2015b) this sense of attunement is captured in "emplaced (*ek-static*) transcendence," where there is the "anticipatory and ecstatic" encounter with nature "experienced as an autonomous and essentially mysterious non-human other that both sustains and is sustained by places—places in which we find ourselves and live out our lives," and for Bonnett, this attunement "foregrounds the notion of transcendence that leads to both a questioning of the anthropocentricism (i.e., its metaphysical basis) that informs many Western moral views and an acknowledgement of intrinsic value in nature" (7). Jardine (2000) also talks of attunement in the form of a "re-awakening" to the Earth in his understanding of "ECOPEDAGOGY," which "is meant to re-awaken a sense of the intimate interconnection between ecological awareness and pedagogy" (47), and for Jardine, "ecological awareness" is inseparable from the *essence of education* (10).

It is crucial to briefly examine Heidegger's (1993b) critique of Sartre's existential humanism, for it will set the stage for the interpretation of nature/Earth in both Jardine and Bonnett. Although certainly not using these precise terms, Heidegger's claim is that Sartre's existentialism is anthropocentric and subjectivist, i.e., it holds the potential to devolve into an irresolvable ethical relativism, and beyond this, Heidegger is critical of the ethical view that rejects the influences of any extraneous influences, and because Sartre sets the human being at the center of the universe, it is the human that forges the world as it makes various choices and in the process "creates" values. This amounts to a vacuous endeavor, for the only "directives" given in Sartre's ethics are subjective in nature, and what is required for the ground and context of authentic human dwelling, according to Heidegger, is an originary sense of *ēthos*, which is given over by Being/Earth. Heidegger (2015) states that the "originary community does not first arise through the taking up of reciprocal relations," through the forming of rules, laws, institutions, and the like, "only society arises this way—rather community *is* through *each individual* being bound in advance to something that binds and determines every individual in exceeding them. Something must be manifest that is neither individual [subjective] taken alone, nor community as such" (74). As stated, for Heidegger, it is Being/Earth, as the phenomenon that stands beyond humans and at once shelters their standing in as a *belonging to*, uniting them and binding them to the future promise of a destiny, the appropriation of which becomes *as* possibility in and through an originary sense of *ēthos*. Thomson (2009) explains that Heidegger endorses "*transcendental* ethical realism," which is "capable of generating" a more acceptable form of *ethical perfectionism*, "one which emphasizes the cultivation of *distinctive* traits of *Dasein*, and so, I will suggest, yields more acceptable ethical consequences" (449). Thomson goes on to add that in Heidegger's view, "we can indeed discover what really matters when we are appropriately open to the environment, but what we thereby discover is neither a 'fact' nor a 'value' but rather a transcendental source of meaning that cannot be reduced to facts, values, or entities of any kind" (448).

Here, we must read carefully, for Heidegger is not suggesting that Being or the Earth (as *primordial mystery*) is granting "ethical directives" in a form consistent with the traditional view of ethics, as a systematic set of rules and principles for judging, determining, and inspiring "good," "excellent," or "moral" behavior. This would be expressive of the Greek notion of *ethike*, in terms of "habituated behaviors"—*ethos* (εθος). Rather, what Heidegger is suggesting is that Being/Earth grants and makes possible the living out of a more primordial and *originary* sense of ethics, which makes any notion or practice of ethics (*ethike*) *derivative* and possible in the first instance. This for Heidegger (1993b) is *ēthos* (ηθος), which indicates a form of dwelling, for the original Greek understanding of the more original sense of *ēthos* bespeaks the human being's "abode, dwelling place," and, as related to the human's participation in Being's *presencing*, it "names the open region in which man [sic] dwells. The open region of his abode allows what pertains to man's essence, and what in thus arriving resides in nearness to him, to appear" (Heidegger, 1993b, 256). And yet what appears is not in the complete control of the human being, therefore it is beyond the subjectivity we encounter in Sartre. Heidegger's understanding of ethics (ηθος) lives beyond voluntarism, and here, as related directly to my concern with *epistemological directionality*, we might also talk of *ontological directionality*, as represented in such claims as "Man is not the lord of beings. Man is the shepherd of Being" (245). Although Heidegger is clear that thinking "accomplishes the relation of Being to the essence of man," it is not the case that thinking creates or causes this relationship, rather thinking "brings this relation to Being solely as something handed over to it from Being" (217). Heidegger provides the following conditions that are necessary for thinking authentically about our ethical comportment, and it is found in the turn toward Being and away from any subject-centered notion of human existence:

> Only in so far as man, ek-sisting into the truth of Being, belongs to Being can there come from Being itself the assignment of those directives that must become law and rule for man. In Greek, to assign is *nemein*. *Nomos* is not only law but more originally the assignment contained in the dispensation of Being. Only the assignment is capable of dispatching man into Being. Only such dispatching is capable of supporting and obliging. (262)

Jardine (1998) relates this difficult notion directly to pedagogy in the following illustration: The teacher is a disciplinarian and authority only because she is already beholden and responsible to a higher authority. For Jardine in order to teach, in order to love children and embrace an authentic pedagogy, this requires "a loving interest in the Earth," and it is the Earth, much like Heidegger's notion of Being, that unites our pedagogical pursuits in terms of an ethical dwelling: "Our adult responsibility for and authority 'over' children is at once a responsibility to the Earth on which we dwell with children. Teaching is, in part, an introduction of our children to the authority of the Earth itself, an authority to which even our authority as adults is secondary" (81), and we might say, dependent and beholden in advance. As related directly to the discussion of Heidegger, Thomson, and original ηθος, Jardine claims that our "obedience, in the face of the archaic authority of the Earth loses its moralistic character and can be finally heard again in its origin—*ab audire*, to listen, to attend, to be attuned" (81). Thus, to reiterate, in relation to *meaning*, there is an *ontological directionality* philosophized by Jardine that accomplishes the de-centering of the human subject because it indicates a change in the way we approach *meaning*, which is more primordial than *epistemology*. The de-centered subject in its relationship to the Earth should now be understood in the following manner: Meaning's Source (*Earth*) ⇒ human (as integral participant in *Source*). For Jardine, the teacher who is authentic, by answering in and through giving herself over to the superior authority of the Earth, "becomes a facilitator, a provocateur, and, one hopes, a joyous *example* of a loving interest in children and in the contours and textures of the Earth" (80).

Ecopedagogy and the integrated curriculum-of-life: The recovery of the earth

The neologism, "ecopedagogy" coined by Jardine (2000), has little or no relation to what is termed "environmental education" in the curriculum as a subject of study. The Earth, Jardine makes clear, must not to be reduced to a "subject of study," it is "precisely *not* a specialized curricular topic" for it is the case that "such specialization unwittingly pretends that the Earth is not underfoot *no matter what*" (Jardine, 1998, 76). There are complex meanings associated with this notion of the Earth (as *terra firma*) beneath our feet, as bearing us up, that will be discussed below. Jardine (2000) is emphatic on the point that we must not allow the Earth to be reduced to yet another "object" of study—as in traditional metaphysics or "philosophy *of* X" approaches, where the *object* of study "becomes precisely this, an object that stands over and against the researcher" (105). We must also resist the temptation to approach the Earth in terms that simply "reverse the polarity" inherent in metaphysical thought, e.g., as found in deep ecological philosophies such as the "Gaia hypothesis," for in attempting to reconceptualize the human's intimate relation to the Earth, Jardine finds it useless to try to "argue against the metaphysical tenet of fragmentation and isolation with another metaphysical tenet of wholeness and relatedness. It is useless because it is precisely proceeding metaphysically that is the problem" (4). Ecopedagogy is an attuned attitude toward and the embodiment of the "intimate interconnection between ecological awareness and pedagogy" (47). This way of living, learning, and teaching expresses a relationship that is not the result of human voluntarism, rather it is a primordial, ontological relationship that bespeaks the interconnectedness between "the sustainable generativities of the earth and the generativity represented by our children and embraced by pedagogy" (47). For Jardine, the interwoven constellations of relations that make up ecopedogogy bespeak the essence of *"education itself,"* which is both deep in character and mood (10).

"Ecopedagogy," according to Jardine, "assumes that there is always and already a deep, ambiguous kinship at work between the real, earthly lives of children, the tasks of pedagogy" (48), and the primordial *mystery* that is bound up with the Earth. Ecology, as conceived by Jardine, considers the conditions that sustain life, and this consideration is "intimately pedagogic at its heart," and the task of pedagogy is to reveal to children the Earth's many ways of granting sustainability, bestowing the ways "required for life to go on in a full and healthy and wholesome and sustainable way" (48). Authentic pedagogy demands the recovery of the Earth from the *oblivion of ontology*. This "recovery" is related to *ontological ecology* and it

> concerns not what we can do (in some utopian, Enlightenment-ideal sense, which is literally no-place), but what is proper, what is properly responsive to the place in which we find ourselves, those actions which have a sense of propriety, those actions which are "fitting," and which issue up out of a place as a considerate response to that place (i.e., a response which somehow acts in accordance with the sustainability of that response). (118)

To properly be "responsive" entails attention to what is bound up with what I have termed *ontological directionality* and *epistemological directionality,* and in Jardine this is expressed in the crucial difference, which is *ontological* in nature, between the human's encounter with and response to the world in terms of either confronting it with the drive to master it as "chaos" or releasing oneself over to it in terms of embracing it as "mystery." It must be noted that "responsiveness" always entails a *responsible* stance, and this stance is determined by "how" the world comes-to-*presence* for our appropriation as it is attuned, or *colored,* by moods that antedate, because they are more primordial than, psychological structures and epistemological categories. "Chaos" is the term for all that stands beyond the periphery of human knowledge, for this view assumes that the "sphere of knowledge is a limited" and the "existence of order is co-extensive with the existence of our knowledge" (118). In and through knowing we give form and order to things, and "anything that stands outside the sphere of our control is precisely *out of control*" (118). Linked with this notion is the view that our comportment is dependent on only what we know, and "we must know everything in order to act with full confidence," or we "must portion out gradations of reliability with the methods of statistics and thereby regain our confidence through the mathematization of our hesitancy regarding what we know" (119). This view is attuned by *metaphysical instrumentalism* and the predicament it creates is one of constantly attempting to either keep chaos at bay or frantically "rushing to usher it into that sphere, because we have come to believe that it is only what we know that we can rely on" (119). Contrarily, to encounter the world in terms of "mystery" requires the re-awakening or re-attunement to understand that although the sphere of human knowledge is inherently limited, all that lies beyond that sphere "contains implicate patters and relationships which have their own integrity, which are not of our own making" (119). This inspires us to act with "propriety," according to Jardine, which is acting with the understanding that "we are connected to and dependent upon that which falls outside of the sphere of knowing," and this inspires a deep sense of *responsibility* for the Earth, which calls for us to "become delicate and careful and attentive to what crackles beyond the boundaries that our knowledge has set" (119).

A kindred notion regarding the responsibility that our relationship to the *ontological mystery* entails, in terms of the primordial power of the Earth/Being, is found in the existential phenomenology of Marcel (1995, 1965, 1950). Marcel makes the distinction between *problem* and *mystery*: a problem, much like the notion of how we attempt to reign in "chaos" via epistemological means and technical machinations, requires an investigation in order to attempt, through the application of one or another method, to solve it by means of offering tentative solutions based on the findings of our investigations. "A problem," writes Marcel (1965), "is something which I meet, which I find complete before me, but which I can therefore lay siege to and reduce" (75). This indeed, according to Jardine, is the way standardized curriculum approaches education in general and students in particular, they are mistakes to be corrected, and, in essence, they are problems to be solved. A mystery, contrarily, as Marcel articulates, "is something in which I myself am involved," and mystery, which is related to ontological *presence* as opposed to a way of being *present* before an object or entity, "transcends every conceivable technique" (75). In the *presence* of a mystery we grasp a sense of our belonging through an "intuition which [we] possess without immediately knowing [ourselves] to possess it—an intuition which cannot be, strictly speaking, self-conscious and which can grasp itself only through modes of experience in which its image is reflected, and which lights up by being thus reflected in them" (79). As Stewart and Mickunas (1990) observe, ultimately, the human's "relation to Being [is] mystery, and although not capable of discursive or rational explanations, it is glimpsed in certain intensely lived situations," and when reflecting on these situations in a phenomenological manner, "these experiences point to the fundamental mystery itself—the mystery of Being" (79–80). Marcel warns, however, that it is "no doubt, always possible to logically and psychologically degrade a mystery so as to turn it into a problem" (79). This represents a "vicious proceeding," because at the center of the *ontological mystery* lies the tragic double-bind, i.e., although it is the "essence" of the mystery "to be recognized or capable of recognition" for our betterment, the possibility exists, to our detriment, that it "may also be ignored and actively denied" (79). For Jardine (2000), this lies at the "heart of the notion of ecopedagogy," for it is possible, even when we are well-informed about so-called "ecological" matters, "to work with full confidence and fully gracious intent in the area of pedagogy and yet betray an unintended ecological insanity," for if the *ontological mystery* is ignored, "we can unintentionally live in a way that works against the real, earthly conditions under which the pedagogy to which we aspire is actually possible" (96).

Jardine's (1998) understanding of the *integrated curriculum* is grounded in a phenomenological view wherein we reveal and catch glimpses of the "previously unnoticed interconnectedness of things hidden beneath the surface analytic assumptions of difference and separateness" (70), which are the underlying views of standardized curriculum concerned with regulating, systematically controlling, and ultimately eliminating the influence of *chaos* in the educational process. This drive for "control" is directed by analytic-empirical curriculum research, which Jardine labels a "disintegrative analytic" method "aimed at rendering education a closed question, aimed at rendering human life lifelessly 'objective' under the glare of knowledge-as-*stasis*" (72). In Jardine's ontological view of *ecology*, every component of the universe represents a "unique center around which all others can be gathered *while at the same time that very [component] rests on the periphery of all others, proximal to some, distant to others*" (70). This indicates that each "thing" is not an individuated self-contained, self-sufficient monad, but rather the *thing* becomes *itself* only in relation to all things that are *not itself* or *other*, and this represents for Jardine, the "paradoxical" sense of "interweaving indebtedness," which is synonymous with a phenomenologically reconceived view of the Earth. It is in and through the authentic understanding of the *integrated curriculum* that the potential recovery of the Earth is possible, and what the *integrated curriculum* reveals is the "way in which the Earth is our abode, our dwelling, and how our lives as teachers are an integral part of that dwelling," and such a re-attuned view of our intimate relation with others as *originary* denizens of the Earth, disrupts "deeply held beliefs and images of understanding, self-understanding and mutual understanding, pointing to a sense of 'inter-relatedness,' 'inter-dependency,' or 'inter-connectedness'" (Jardine, 1998, 72).

Integration, as Jardine conceives of it, is not to be mistaken for the commonly held educational theory of "curriculum integration" as the cross-curricular organization of similarly "themed" units of study, as in multidisciplinary and interdisciplinary approaches to integration that stress skills such as literacy, critical thinking, numeracy, and research techniques (Drake & Burns, 2004). For Jardine (1998), "integration" is an ontological, ecological, and deeply spiritual matter that is attuned and informed by the Earth, which reveals "glimpses of a truly lived curriculum, a true *curriculum vitae*, one that leads to generativity, movement, liveliness, and difficulty that lies at the heart of our lives" (73). Much like Heidegger's (1968) notion of *meditative thought* in its relation to the "truth of Being," or *that-which-regions*, the *integrated curriculum* reveals to us the ontological relationship between human thought and the Earth, wherein the *epistemological directionality* of *metaphysical instrumentalism* is overturned. Because this relationship we enter into is attuned through a sense of "wonder" (*thaumazein*), as I have already introduced, we transcend the commonplace understanding that views *meaning* and *meaningfulness* as moving from human ⇒ world ⇒ *meaning* to the renewed and enlightened understanding of Meaning's Source (*Earth*) ⇒ human (as integral participant in *Source*). Jardine refers to this radical change in *epistemological directionality*, which is grounded in ontology, as bringing knowledge "down to Earth," but knowledge in this reconceived view is *grounded*

> not only in the epistemological sense, but in the moist, fleshy sense of given earthliness, given *humus*, made human...We may have to admit that the continued existence of our lives and the lives of our children contain an

Earthen darkness and difficulty—an Earthen life—that we have heretofore fantasized out of curricular existence. The integrated curriculum, understood out from under these celibate fantasies, requires a recovery of the delicate, interweaving, and intertwining *humus* of a *curriculum vitae*; it requires a recovery of the Earth. (76)

Jardine (1998) is adamant on the point that "epistemic excellence," "grade point averages," and students' "mastery of requisite skills" are never fundamental elements within an authentic education. Rather, the *essence of education* lies in the ontological understanding of the *integrated curriculum*, which awakens educators to the view that English, Science, and Math are never mere disciplines or subjects of "study," but are ways that sustain "quite literally" our ability to live as teachers, students, and human beings on the Earth, for it is only through our "ability *be* on an Earth" that our lives will be sustained (75). For example, the *integrated* Language Arts curriculum always "depends," not on testable theories for writing and reading comprehension, but rather an *Earthen literacy* that understands that the language arts curriculum *is* already a *curriculum-of-life* (*curriculum vitae*), which proceeds "as a living response to the living, deeply dependant intricacies that pertain to that classroom" as those activities are already mediated by the ontological *presence* of the Earth (Jardine, 2000, 52). For the authentic "life of language occurs in the tensive, mediated interplays between forms and disciplines and established wisdoms of/in language and the newly erupting voices of the young," and this interplay of life's "integrated" components, emerges only in and through our connections to and conversations with the Earth, and these relations, "*depend upon one another,* and each finds both its (re)source and its limit in its opposite" (51). Regarding the science curriculum, Jardine points out that it can never be merely an issue of teaching "ecology" as a subject, for the integrated nature of our Earthly relationships as manifest in the science curriculum already embody the "long-standing images of ourselves, images of the earth and our place and standing in its ways, the need for ecological responsibility, and the images of nature, limits, and necessities of human understanding" (88).

Concerning mathematics, which for Jardine (1998) speaks the language of *humility,* educators must be awakened to the understanding that a "thorough 'grounding' in mathematics is of little use if that knowledge is understood in such a way that there is no longer any *real* ground that is safe to walk. Mathematics must become *earthen* in how it is understood, how it is taught, and how it is 'grounded'" (75). It is possible for us, and in some cases it is academically necessary, to "'draw' the boundaries for the teaching of mathematics as a curricular subject," however, this is not, as Jardine is careful to point out, the equivalent of "*giving*" or imposing a boundary on mathematics, for this would "prevent it from intertwining with our lives and the life of the Earth" (75). According to Jardine, teaching mathematics to children is a supreme expression of "teaching a love of the earth on which the teaching and learning and savoring of mathematics is actually possible" (75). Jardine (2000) provides the reader with a wonderfully descriptive and moving example of how this *earthly* notion of mathematics unfolds within our intimate encounters with the natural world, in moments when we slow down our pace and open our ears and hearts to the call of the Earth, and in doing so, releasing ourselves over to its *primordial* address, we hear the multivocal resonances or soundings of the past and present heralding the *futural* voices that require our immediate attention. Here, in this passage, Jardine asks us to contemplate

> the deep pleasures to be had in mathematical symmetries and geometric curves of just [a] yellow leaf corkscrewing down from a late fall Cottonwood, and how it heralds the arc of seasons and the movements of the planets and sun, and the bodily desires for shelter, and how many have stood here like this, stock still, trying to read the deep patterns and dignities and eloquences of this place. (14)

As this poetic description intimates, linking the above reading of Jardine with teaching and an ontological view of ecology that has been argued, pedagogy is an ecological and spiritual matter. It is grounded in the *re-awakening* and *recognition* (re-attunement) of our indebtedness to the Earth. In such "ecologically" informed "recognition," Jardine (1998) claims that we understand that the "natality that springs from this original blessing of the Earth and lies at the heart of education" (74) cannot be ignored without perpetuating and intensifying the ever-widening blight of ecological disaster. I now move to relate Jardine's ontological concern for the Earth and its "potentialities and possibilities" to Heidegger's reading of the work of art and Hölderlin's poetry, and it raises the philosophical concern of "how the deep and moist interweavings and integrity of the Earth is both an original constraint on our lives, but also an original blessing, an original freedom, the overstepping of which pushes the Earth beyond what is possible for it to sustain" (74).

It is certainly plausible to interpret Jardine's notion of the *integrated curriculum* in terms that are relatable to Heidegger's later philosophy of the "fourfold". For example, Jardine, inspired by a Japanese song, *Koku*

Reibo, writes of the phenomenon of a *bell ringing in the empty sky*. Jardine insists that the "sky is not a vacuum to be filled. It is not *filled* with the sound of the bell" (91). Rather, the sky is empty in the sense of transcending any definitive and concretized sense of "identity," for it "empties out into all things without exception, it summons up an intimate, enclosed indebtedness to the whole of the Earth" (91). The bell ringing in the empty sky embodies "the interconnectedness of all things," which ultimately reveals, as related to the *integrated curriculum* that any and all things require "everything else in order to exist" (88). We indeed find this kindred notion in Heidegger's (1971) reading of the *jug* as a "thing" that is nested within a context, or relational web of references, that allow it to be as it *is*, i.e., to allow the thing's *thingness* to manifest in terms of its *own self-presencing*. Thus, Heidegger's analysis is concerned with the thing's ontological *presence* as opposed to it *being present-at-hand*, for its *originary presence* lives only because it is interwoven into the ontological referential structure of Earth, Sky, Mortals, and Divinities: "The thing things. Thinging gathers. Appropriating the fourfold, it gathers the fourfold's stay, its while, into something that stays for a while: into this thing, that thing" (174). It is the mirror-play (*Spiel*) between the fourfold that sets each into their own essence while at once determining the "play that betroths each of the four to each through the enfolding clasp of their mutual appropriation" (179). For none of the four "insists on its own particularity. Rather, each is expropriated, within their mutual appropriation, into its own being," and, as related to Jardine's *integrated curriculum*,

> [e]ach of the four mirrors in its own way the presence of the others...The mirroring, lighting each of the four, appropriates their own presencing into simple belonging to one another. Mirroring in this appropriating-lighting way, each of the four plays to each of the others. The appropriative mirroring sets each of the four free into its own, but it binds these free ones into the simplicity of their essential being towards one another. (179)

Although there are undeniable similarities between the philosophies of Jardine and Heidegger present to this above description, I argue that the understanding of the Earth in Jardine's essays is consistent with Heidegger's (2015, 1993b) understanding of the Earth in the "Origin of the Work of Art" (1935–1936) and the Hölderlin lecture course, *Germania and der Rhine* (1934–1935), and not Heidegger's (1971) later understanding of Earth in "The Thing," which is the "building bearer, nourishing with its fruits, tending to water and rock, plant and animal" (178). In the "Origin of the Work of Art," Heidegger (1993b) introduces, in addition to the reconceived concept of "world," the term "Earth," and these counter-striving forces are two essential features of art's ability to give, grant, and bestow meaning in Dasein's existence. Much like Heidegger in the 1930s, Jardine thinks the Earth in terms of radical limitations, primordial concealment, and *mystery*, which Heidegger philosophizes in terms of the "abyss," or *Ab-grund*, which is literally an Earth that is most properly without ground and this calls for the temporary establishment of "ground" and subsequent efforts to give new "ground"—this endeavor, in the most *originary* sense, instantiates the "difficult" process of learning. Indeed, for Jardine (1998), the Earth continually "disrupts" our deeply held beliefs and images we hold fast to, for listening and responding to the Earth is often "difficult, perhaps painful" because it is forever "disruptive of the clear and distinct boundaries we have set for ourselves and our children" (78). In addition, Jardine, in terms consistent with Heidegger, also understands the Earth as the *terra firma* or soil from out of which we spring, upon which we build our dwellings, and to which we return in death—for the Earth is "moist," "fleshy," and it is *humus*. Finally, when Jardine weaves Heidegger into his essays, the philosophy comes from Heidegger's productive period during the mid-1930s, where the Earth is linked inextricably to because it is synonymous with the *primordial ontological phenomenon of concealment—as mystery*. The Earth "gives" or "grants" in these readings only in and through its withdrawal into finitude (Magrini, 2010).

Earth for Heidegger is the radicalization of *physis* as the coming-into-presence-of-beings in his thinking on the *Ereignis*, the historical revelation and appropriation of Dasein's historical destiny. The Earth for Heidegger, much like Jardine, is also the supreme spiritual presence, a sublime, inexplicable holy force that is beyond even the gods. The Earth is derived from and equated with Hölderlin's notion of "divine Nature," and Heidegger argues that "world" cannot be thought of outside its connection to the Earth, world cannot exist or arise without it. Dasein cannot dwell authentically without acknowledging its debt to the Earth, for Dasein's Being belongs to the Earth, which represents the divine-spiritual aspects of the holy, a force Dasein must return to in order to transform its life. The Earth represents the awe-inspiring sublimity of nature, which rises and exceeds humanity. The Earth shows itself authentically (opening the possibility for *originary* ηθος) when *presencing* in an undisclosed and inexplicable manner (*as* mystery), demonstrating the essence of existence as a self-concealing phenomenon, a phenomenon of double-concealment. The Earth *is* primordial concealment, which grounds the secondary mode of concealment, the dissembling in which phenomena presence in deceptively curious ways. For this reason, Jardine (1998) claims that "our lives and the lives of our children" will always contain, as a primordial and *originary* way of Being-in the-world, "an Earthen darkness and difficulty—an Earthen life that we have heretofore fantasized out of curriculum existence" (76). Dasein first comes into its Being, first approaches its self-understanding, by measuring itself against the awesome powers of the Earth, for destiny is grounded in precisely the things that Dasein does not and cannot know, grounded in that which is never mastered with confidence (Magrini, 2010). Heidegger contemplates the importance of Earth as related to Dasein as a historical being, philosophizing the Earth in terms of historical ground, in relation to Temporality and finitude, as the Holy force that shatters Dasein's individuation. This returns us to Jardine's notion of "disruption" and the need for us to continually establish new grounds all the while demonstrating the responsibility of guardians who are bound to something that is beyond us, that is transcendent, and yet we are an intimate part of it—it is from this authority, the authority of the Earth, that we first gain human, or *humane,* authority:

> In the Earth's becoming homeland, it opens itself to the power of the gods... Where the Earth manifests herself in the disinterestedness of authentic Dasein, she is holy—holy Earth. The holy one, the abyss in which firmness and individualness of all grounds retreats and where everything yet finds its way to a constantly dawning new beginning. (Heidegger, 2015, 69)

Nature as "self-arising" phenomenon: An education in discovering the intrinsic value inherent in nature

Bonnett (2007) argues that the concern for nature *should* be education's primary concern: "[E]ducation in general should have at [its] heart the ambition to bring a range of searching questions concerning nature to the attention of learners, and to encourage them to develop their own on-going responses to those questions" (709). However, such questions are foreign to curriculum and the "re-focusing" of its concerns, which inspire such deep and ontological questions ("original questions") regarding nature, will not come easily. This is because "raising such questions can be inhibited by denying the language in which they can be meaningfully articulated," and this occurs in one way when nature is dismissed "as simply a social construct that has no objective reality and is redolent with ideological bias" (709). Underlying such a view, as has been discussed, is the *scientific-technical* attunement of Western metaphysics, or the "metaphysics of mastery," which, according to Bonnett (2013), "vitiates proper engagement with the natural environment in particular, by subverting sensitivity to its own normative and purposive character" (187). This view represents a pernicious form of humanism that is anthropocentric and instrumental, reducing nature to either a mechanical causal nexus or non-human "resource" that is there for the taking in and through the devices of human machination. When nature is set radically apart from the human, and thought to be a "product of our categories, theories, narratives, and texts," when it is taken to be "purely physical matter/energy operating according to blind universal laws" with "no internal significances," nature, is therefore "incapable of possessing inherent intrinsic value" (Bonnett, 2015b, 2). At a fundamental level, these and other positions that view nature as fully understandable in technical, scientific, and mathematical terms are grounded in what Bonnett terms "scientism," which is a view that

> scientific thinking should be the arbiter of good thinking as a whole and it holds a privileged position when it comes to identifying and investigating fundamental questions concerning the nature of reality—what constitutes it and what measures are necessary to effect "human progress". (2013, 192)

In line with my position, Bonnett (2015b) is acutely critical of the manner in which "scientism" plays out in contemporary curriculum and education, for it is "evidenced in the broad context of education in espousals of aiming at outcomes that are observable and measurable, in seeing the curriculum in terms of pre-specified objectives that can be clearly delineated and 'delivered'" (3). This view is a result of what I have already identified as the attunement of *metaphysical instrumentalism* in Chapter 2, and Bonnett (2013) shares this view, which he couches in terms of "cultural framing". Framing, much like deep moods (*Stimmungen*) from out of which we see, interpret, understand, and talk about our world, determines "how things are described, hence, what is visible and what remains invisible; what is relevant and important and what is not; what is a problem and what is not; what counts as a valid way of proceeding in addressing a problem and what does not" (189). It is necessary to note, in relation to what I have argued throughout, most particularly in terms of the world-*as*-picture in Heidegger's critique of technology, that the "deepest and most pervasive framings install us into a particular version of reality—that is to say they operate as metaphysics" (190). Bonnett is quite correct to view this in terms of a problem with the language we use to describe our intimate phenomenological relationship with nature, which is really the search for a language capable of breaking "the spell of the things that are present by naming the things that are absent" (191), or those things that defy a spatial-temporal presence, or being *present-at-hand* before us in scientific-mathematical terms.

This is at once related to a "perceived" problem inherent within phenomenological inquiry, e.g., the persistent criticism that phenomenology is reducible to subjective "introspection" (Dennett, 1991) and its language is at best literary or poetic in character, and at worst, utterly meaningless. Indeed Bonnett (2007) makes us aware of this when stating that often times the language phenomenology incorporates when describing the human's ontological relationship with nature is labeled "purely academic, esoteric, even frothy" (709). Marcel (1950) addresses this precise concern when speaking about our ontological relationship with the world and others, which manifests in terms of a palpable and very real *presence*. It is interesting to note that Marcel provides examples of such transcendent experiences in terms of our intimate encounters with others, works of art, and landscapes wherein we are surrounded by nature's sublime and transcendent mystery as *presence* (52). As discussed in Chapter 2, referencing Diagnault's (1992) definition of the *simulacra of curriculum*, it is often the case that we *forget* that simulacra are composed of nothing other than the residue of lived experience, drawing their power from primordial modes of lived experience. In this act of "forgetting," according to Marcel (1950), lived experience and the ontological aspects of our lives are devalued, relegated to the inferior status of mere "secondary" and inconsequential ways of being. The danger exists that when we attempt to communicate a deeply and profoundly moving lived, ontological experience of nature, and this for Marcel is the experience of "transcendence," we are dealing with an "idea fundamentally incommunicable, an idea which we cannot even communicate in its pure essence to ourselves" (52). Thus, there is "always the risk of the hardened, transmissible expression of the illumination growing over the illumination like a sort of shell and gradually taking its place" (52–53). Phenomenology recognizes this linguistic and conceptual difficulty in communicating "transcendent" experiences, for when attuned by *metaphysical instrumentalism* ("metaphysics of mastery"), we tend to believe that

> the initial living experience could survive only on condition of degrading itself to a certain extent, or rather shutting itself up in its own simulacrum; but this simulacrum, which should only be there on sufferance, as a kind of *locum tenens*, is always threatening to free itself from its proper subordinate position and to claim a kind of independence to which it has no right; and the serious danger to which thought itself is exposed is that of starting off from the simulacrum, as an existing basis, instead of referring itself perpetually to that invisible and gradually less and less palpable presence, to indicate which (and to recall it to our memories) is the sole justification of the simulacrum...philosophy of the past [Western metaphysics]...has been built up not on experience but on a waste product of experience that had taken experience's name. (53–54)

It is crucial to note, as Bonnett (2015b, 2013, 2007, 2004) points out, and, as we saw, Jardine is also aware of this, even views that inspire deep "ecological" movements seeking to "preserve" nature or the planet operate out of the framing that "is deeply corrosive of our relationship with the world," which is grounded, as stated, in a "highly pervasive metaphysics of mastery," and this "arrogant instrumentality that this entails hollows out our relationship to what is present" (Bonnett, 2013, 191). Even what Bonnett (2004) terms "bio-centric views" harbor a latent anthropocentrism, and while they "may be suggestive of important alternative attitudes...they lack the intellectual resources to replace it" (114). The problem with such views, as I discuss below in terms of "sustainable development," is that they are focused on changing the environment and not the human being, and what is required is a change of the human being's attunement, which opens the potential for the re-establishment of the "legitimacy of modes of thinking and being that the metaphysics of mastery occludes" (Bonnett, 2013, 192). For example, the ecological philosophy of "sustainable development" is grounded in the utilitarian principle of posterity (*the problem of posterity*), which adopts the view that we *should* develop the earth in such a way that resources meet our present needs without compromising the planet in such a way that future generations are unable to meet their needs. Sustainable development is a very seductive notion as, on a generous interpretation, it seems to marry two highly desired goals: first, the idea of conserving those aspects of nature that are valued (i.e., in some sense "needed") but that are currently endangered by human agency; secondly, the idea of accommodating ongoing human aspirations to "develop" that is, in some sense to have more or better. (Bonnett, 2007, 710)

Although this view appeals to both "enlightened captains of industry" and "eco-warriors," there is an inherent problem with it: when questions and concerns regarding *what is sustained, at what level, over what time span,* or concerns with *whose needs are being met, how they are prioritized, according to what criteria,* the answers and responses, when provided, "are highly contestable" (710). This is because sustainable development embraces "anthropocentric and economic motives that lead to nature being seen as essentially a *resource,* an object to be intellectually possessed and physically manipulated and exploited in whatever ways are perceived to suit (someone's version of) human needs and wants" (710). Thus, sustainable development might be understood as yet another version of the technical-scientific *will to power,* the goal of which is the mastering of nature in the present as well as the future with the sole purpose of sustaining the human race and insuring its progress. Here, with "humanistic hubris, nature is constantly to be challenged, set in order, re-engineered, etc., to meet human needs—and often, not even this, but merely human convenience" (710). Since the aims of sustainable development are instrumental and anthropocentric, primarily grounded in a scientific view of the world (that is expressed as "scientism"), what is missing or occluded in this view, since it is primarily concerned with knowledge as the means by which to master and exploit the world for human resources, is a grounding ontological fundament. In addition, although couched in terms of utilitarian ethics, sustainable development smuggles in a scientific epistemological view that severely limits the scope of what counts as "valid" knowledge. If there is to be an understanding of nature that is transcendent, then a phenomenological approach is needed, which for Bonnett is the ontological approach to understanding nature as a transcendent phenomenon, and it is to Bonnett's unique ontology of nature that I now turn.

Bonnett (2004) argues, "Nature as the self-arising does constitute our primordial reality," and as the self-arising, it "stands as something whose origins are independent of us and as a domain that we need properly to apprehend of we are to understand our environment and our place in it" (40). In Bonnett, just as in Jardine, we encounter a view of nature grounded in an ontological understanding of *nature*, and not a view of the "environment" in terms of either the "natural environment" or "human environment," within which we dwell. Nature is antecedent to any conceptions of the "environment," and, here too, the view of Ontology NOT Epistemology is embraced. Indeed, Bonnett (2007) refers to nature in terms of an *"epistemological mystery,"* for although "we may on occasion feel ourselves to be intimately involved" with nature, and for that reason believe that nature might be "intimately known," this is not the case. Since nature is "self-arising" and radically *other*, it "can never be fully known" or "intellectually possessed" (713). Bonnett (2015b) focuses on three elements that are crucial to understanding the ontology of nature as "transcendent": its inherent otherness, mysteriousness, and intrinsic integrity. The third of these features are discussed below, but my immediate remarks shall focus on nature's radical alterity and its tendency towards concealment as *primordial mystery*. Nature is transcendent in that it is inherently *other*, primordially it is before and beyond our intentions, and although we affect it in various ways, we never determine it. Thus, although nature shows up or *presences* for us, we are not the sole authors of what we experience, and it is hence impossible for us to know this experience from the inside (Bonnett, 2013). Nature's ambiance is something that we are affected by, but we do not project. Nature comes to meet us when we are receptive in and through the consecrated act of releasing ourselves over to it, and in this way, through the encounter with nature as transcendent, our Being is enlivened and animated. "To acknowledge this element of transcendence is to re-admit fluidity and mystery into the environment that can gift inspiration and lead us to new insights" (196).

Transcendence is also linked with nature's mysteriousness—we can never fully know it—it is beyond complete epistemological justification (Bonnett, 2015b, 6). According to Bonnett, any attempts to fully possess nature through various and sundry technical and scientific machinations, destroys its essence. In fact, nature shows itself in so many diverse ways through innumerable experiences that we can only hope to know a limited amount of things about it. As related to my earlier remarks regarding primordial concealment, there are always elements and facets of nature's "self-showing" that remain concealed and thus defy full disclosure. Nature, for the most part, is recalcitrant in the face of human understanding. Bonnett reminds us that due to the radical limitations bounding the human condition, our thought is incapable of fully encompassing the smallest and most fragile flower, let alone grasping the intricacies of the unfolding of massive and distant galaxies. In short, as Bonnett observes, no matter how advanced our technology, "there remains a nature, an order, recognized as external [*other*] to our will and with which we have to deal and find an accommodation" (5).

Bonnett's notion of nature as "self-rising" might be understood as relating to Heidegger's (1977) description of *physis*, which is normally translated as "nature." Heidegger, however, focuses attention on the sense of the infinitival associated with the Greek understanding of the term, which describes and names the "process of nature's unfolding," as the ever-renewed activity of *concealment* ↔ *unconealment*, in terms of a *poietic* mode of "bringing-forth" (10). Physis, according to Heidegger, is *poiesis* "in the highest sense," as the unaided bringing-forth, "the arising of something out of itself," e.g., "the bursting blossom into bloom, in itself (*en heauton*)" (10). This notion of unaided bringing-forth is contrasted with the artist, whose mode of "bringing-forth" has the "bursting open belonging to bringing-forth not in itself, but in another" (11). Nature, in its essence, is the supreme mode of "truth-happening" (*aletheuien*), for "bringing-forth comes to pass only in so far as something concealed comes into unconcealment. This coming rests and moves freely within what we call revealing (*das Entbergen*)" (11). It is crucial to note, as Lovitt (1977) points out, Heidegger's use of the German word *Entbergen*, formed from the verb *bergen*, the meaning of which is beyond indicating a change from one state to the another, for it also connotes "an opening out from protective concealing, a harboring forth," and this relates to "Heidegger's central tenet that it is only as protected and preserved—and that means as enclosed and secure—that anything is set free to endure, to continue as that which it is, i.e., to be" (11). This indicates that for Heidegger, as connected to *physis*, that the bringing-forth, which is a *poietic* revealing, a "self-arising" letting be seen as this or that thing, is the "protected" emergence of phenomena from out of a primordial mode of concealment (*mystery—finitude*). Nature, in a sense, provides security and guardianship for that which *comes-to-presence*. This might be related to Bonnett's (2004, 2013, 2015b) notion of nature's *nobility* and *intrinsic sense of integrity*.

Bonnett's (2004, 2013, 2015b) phenomenology broaches the issue of value and the normativity of the natural world, and his claim is that nature is intrinsically valuable. It is possible, according to Bonnett (2013), "to experience nature as a transcendent other that warrants respect and possesses inherent intrinsic value, awareness of which should be an integral part of our moral sensitivity" (194). With this claim, problems immediately arise. For example, if the valuing subject is necessary for the condition that there is value, the value itself is at once granted by the valuing subject and related directly back to that subject in a way that "makes the value of a thing a function of its meeting the needs of the valuer" (Bonnett, 2004, 81). This is consistent with the normative view that value is not internal to objects, rather value is based in *relational properties*, and this indicates that in some sense the value is bestowed or *conferred*, "and only entities that function at a certain level of self-consciousness can confer value" (81). Thus, as opposed to "intrinsic" value we have a view to "derivative intrinsic worth," which appears to be "instrumental" in its essence—"nature is being valued for its use—for what it does for the valuer, rather than what it is in itself" (81). This discussion raises an interesting concern regarding our viewing "aspects of non-human nature as objectively [intrinsically] having their own ends that need to be respected, and possessing properties whose value may be recognized by humans, though they are not the source (conferrers) of it" (83).

Bonnett's response is that the immediate experience of the natural world, i.e., "the direct contact with primeval nature unshaped by human hand—the element of authentic naturalness—is value in itself" (87). When demanding *justification* for the claim that nature is intrinsically valuable, Bonnett offers a powerful response that emerges from the phenomenological view that draws on the "lived" moments of our experience with/of nature. There are instances in our "lived" experience of the natural world wherein we simply "feel" and "intuit" either the "rightness" or "wrongness" concerning the ways we are behaving toward, or better, the ways that we are being responsive to nature. For example, we simply feel either the "rightness" or "wrongness" of certain ways of interacting with nature, i.e., we *intuit* the "wrongness" and the accompanying sense of "outrage" at the "despoliation of a sea shore and the sickly movement of the waves covered by an oil slick," or when we *recognize* the need to avoid the "unnecessary trampling of the bluebells emerging through the woodland floor, or the wanton destruction of an ancient oak," and this ambiance of normativity, of value, transcends the subjective valuer, as it "emanates form the things themselves" (2015b, 6–7). In response to critics, Bonnett (2004) asks,

> [I]s not this requirement to give some further justification for a value that we do in fact hold another example of modern rationality exhibiting its own

instrumental orientation— its inherent calculative motive? Why should we allow it to impose this orientation on our understanding of nature? Why should we accept its dictate that our valuing is inadequate if it cannot be formulated in calculative terms? This sort of rationalist objection simply begs the issue at stake. All fundamental intrinsic values rightly are resistant to this requirement and properly demand that rationality be subservient to what they intuit— helping to reveal them more fully by working *within* their ambience. (88)

Bonnett (2015b) informs us that when we sense the nobility and integrity of nature, we are experiencing and relating to an "overriding presence" that shows itself as "mysterious and other, the occasions of such awareness can be the very points at which they arise for us in their 'thisness', *haecceitas,* and we enter into a relationship with them, perhaps developing an incipient sense of something existentially shared—such as a world" (8). It is possible to experience the integrity of nature by bearing witness to the

intricate and complex integration of functioning systems whether it is that of a ciliate protozoan or the human brain. Similarly, a wilderness landscape or natural phenomenon such as the emerging stars at dusk, the play of sunlight on the surf of breaking waves on the shore, the wild but seemingly orchestrated dance of leaves and branches caught in a strong breeze. (6)

Due to nature's radical alterity, although we can never hope to understand fully the intricacies of its highly complex and seemingly unfathomable internal ordering, we can "nonetheless be impressed," indeed be struck and enraptured by the re-awakening and transformative "mood" of wonder (thaumazein), "with a sense of what constitutes the integrity and well-being of natural things, what might count as their fulfillment, and the need for this to be respected" (6). The unity of nature, when approached ontologically, as transcendent, is clearly not "discursive, not that of abstract laws, but something felt in the presencing of things: Their standing forth, showing of themselves" (7). To experience in a phenomenological manner nature in terms of its own self-*presencing,* or self-arising, things are most primordially understood, and in this regard "nature does not dissemble," for it possesses the "nobility of being itself" (9). To experience the integrity of nature is to be attuned to the understanding that we live and inhabit, or more appropriately, dwell in nature in such a way that we allow "normativity" to live, in terms of its *self-presencing,* in the encounter, rather than as the result of ratiocination, and allowing such experiences to stand as such (i.e., as genuinely revelatory, as against explaining them away as, say, merely our projections of some essentially inert reality) opens us up to a world where transcendent powers are in play whose significance far outruns any scientific explanation. Birth, death, movement and stillness, sound and silence, and lightening and darkening are as much constitutive of human experience as, say, Newtonian gravity or Kant's categories of understanding, and sensitivity to them connects us to the cosmos...in a substantive way that neither such Kantian theory nor systematic accounts of the cosmos, whether it be evolution or string theory, ever can. (Bonnett, 2013, 194)

Nature as transcendent *other*, as primordial mystery, which instantiates nobility and purposive integrity, stands as the supreme ontological authority that is beyond us, which indicates for Bonnett that we must listen to nature's reticent demands and directives in order to authentically begin to establish the limits of and criteria for determining what human responses are proper, what actions are ethical, what forms of dwelling are most fitting for humans. "The elemental powers that run through [nature], sensitivity and responsiveness to which connects us to the cosmos and provides the fundament of our lives," and this guides and frames our responses, i.e., the properly limited and respectful ways in which we "participate in shaping the places in which we live and that part constitute us through the anticipative claims that they make on us" (2015b, 9). Nature's integrity is central to its intrinsic worth, and we should at once understand that the loss of "the integrity of the self-arising" signals the loss of human worth, for without nature as an ontological, transcendent phenomenon, serving as a crucial "point of reference, our 'understanding' spins into the free-floating vacuity of a hyper-reality" (Bonnett, 2004, 88).

The attuned educational experience of nature: Tarrying on a woodland path and learning earthen lessons from the birds and the cicadas

As introduced earlier, Bonnett (2015a) claims that in the "lived experience" of nature a form of "human" transcendence occurs, when nature is experienced as an "autonomous and essentially mysterious non-human other that both sustains and is sustained by places—places in which we find ourselves and live out our lives" (7). In this mode of transcendence, he claims, we are re-awakened in such a way that it leads to "both a questioning of the anthropocentrism (i.e., its metaphysical basis)...and an acknowledgement of intrinsic value in nature" (7). Jardine (2000) also believes human transcendence in the face of the Earth will change us for the better by revealing the "ecological entrails implicit *in our pedagogy* itself and the working out of a pedagogy that is more ecologically generous and sustainable, deeply linked to the earth's 'limits of necessity and mystery'"(95), which ultimately opens a view into the ontology of "*education itself*, in its attention to all the disciplines that make up schooling...conceived as deeply ecological in character and mood" (9). Above I talked of nature as transcendent and now I discuss human transcendence as it is bound up with the experience of nature. However, prior to detailing Bonnett's notion of "emplaced (*ek-static*) transcendence" in relation to Jardine's *birding lessons and teachings of the cicadas,* I want to briefly explore a notion of human transcendence in the existential phenomenology of Marcel (1950), who I have referenced throughout. This will prove helpful in understanding transcendence in relation to transcendent nature as an *originary* and ontological way of Being-in-the-world.

Transcendence is the changing or substituting of one experience for another that is grounded in an original ontological stretching out toward the condition of human understanding that is inspired by the "need" or *exigent* "demand" that manifests as the deep, solicitous ontological concern for our Being. We must understand transcendence in a spiritual and affective sense and not a cognitive and epistemological sense. Transcendence, for Marcel, is the basic *exigence ontologique* providing the sense (*Sinn*)-meaning/giving structure to the human condition. This original *demand*, or what Marcel (1950) calls "exigency," which carries a stronger sense in the French than the English equivalent "need" (Anderson, 2006), is not the *demand* to "go beyond all experience whatsoever, but to substitute one mode of experience for another, or, more accurately still, to strive towards an increasingly pure mode of experience" (47). The experience of transcendence for Marcel is relatable to my earlier talk of the transformative powers of moods (*Stimmungen*), for he states that transcendence is the substituting of "one center" of Being for another center and never simply a change in the way we think, for "'thought' is not quite the right word" for understanding transcendence, this is because "we are dealing with a change of attitude of a human being considered as a whole, and with that change, also, in so far as it embodies itself in that human being's acts" (49).

The key feature of "emplaced transcendence" is that it is rooted and grounded in our experience of nature, and thus it is "immediate rather than abstract and discursive," and the experience "opens up a world where transcendent powers are in play whose significance far outruns any scientific explanations" (Bonnett, 2013, 194). Scientism, as a cultural frame, can be overturned, it can be outstripped as we glide from one attunement to another, and this occurs as we enter realms that are embodied and emplaced. Indeed, Bonnett states that in this "emplacement the 'presencing' of each thing is ontologically related to/affected by the presencing of others" (10). This form of emplacement demands a perceptual or intuitional receptivity to the various addresses and the proper sets of responses that comprise the *originary* conversations between nature and the human being. This "conversation" is grounded in an ongoing sense of "mutual anticipation" in that our in-dwelling in nature, as discussed earlier, places demands on us that can, if we are open to it, "determine incisively how and who we are when we are present there" (11), and this indicates that "normativity" and "values" reside inherently in those places of our dwelling, and indeed shape our Being-in-the-world and instill a deep sense of responsibility for our decisions regarding the stances we take amid nature.

The dwelling-space is a context situated in the midst of nature's unfolding, as "self-arising" phenomenon, claimed by the "transcendent qualities of otherness, mystery, and integrity and the open receptive-responsive attitude" (12). This anticipatory attitude is crucial for human transcendence, which must be understood in terms of an *ek-static* state, or better, "event," which, from the Greek *ekstasis,* we understand the sense of "displacement" or what is a "standing outside" oneself and the present place, moment, or mode of attunement. However, this phenomenon must not be understood in terms of somehow transcending of all experience, as Marcel points out, and we must also be cautious when talking of displacement, for Bonnett's entire phenomenology is centered on stressing the sheer rootedness and inextricability of the human being in the dwelling-space or place of nature. The notion of "standing-out" in Bonnett's conception of *ek-static transcendence* is indicative of the ontological relationship with nature that is one of *mutual anticipation,* which it is possible to be strongly aware of, e.g.,

> the sense of anticipation experienced when the walker sets off on a fine spring morning, open to the unknown that is to come—the sights, the smells, the textures, the ambiences and surprises, of say, different places and times of

day. The keen attentiveness of which this speaks quickens life, gives a heightened sense of being. We are enlivened by this capacity to be beyond ourselves [ek-static/transcendence] that enables felt encounters with what is other. (11)

For Bonnett (2013), it is the re-awakening attunement that we experience through "emplaced (*ek-static*) transcendence" that foregrounds our reinterpreted view of the "environment" and subsequently paves the way for the authentic understanding of an "ecological education," in terms that resist and are indeed beyond the "metaphysics of mastery." For the problem exists, as defined in terms of *social efficiency ideology* in curriculum, that under the "the aegis of a persuasive and tacit scientism, schools are in danger of becoming places that require students and teachers both to participate in an environment and to commit to goals that are deeply alienating environmentally" (195). This change of attunement as outlined might be understood in terms of an *originary* form of "learning," which is grounded not in theoretical formulas or conceptual schemas, but in an affective or intuitive awareness of our participation in and contribution to facilitating, establishing, and reestablishing the grounds of our dwelling-space on the Earth.

Jardine (2000), in a wonderfully inspired vignette, describes in highly poetic terms an issue that Bonnett has eloquently philosophized and I have attempted to articulate, namely, that we can and must *learn from nature*. In a deep wooded place in Southern Ontario, a dwelling-space that Jardine had not visited in many years, he reflects and presents through rich phenomenological description, the valued lessons that the woods, the bird-watchers, and the birds have taught and continue to teach him along with the memories that the cicadas in the trees inspire through their natural ability as "archaic storytellers." Much like all "good storytellers," Jardine observes, they tell stories of a life forgotten—a life lived "of deep, fleshy, familial relations that worm their ways out of my belly and breath into these soils, these smells, this air. And I am left shocked that they know so much, that they remember so well, and that they can be so perfectly articulate" (134). In Jardine's phenomenological description, we encounter a form of learning that is ontological and viable, which does not require didactic techniques, primers on ecological science, or computer learning programs focused on instructing students in environmental-friendly "Green" etiquette, and in this instance, it does not even require an *Audubon Bird Identification Guide*. Rather, what it requires is the desire, or better, the openness and releasement—*Gelassenheit* in Heidegger—towards the things that are on the approach, because they are "brought forth," and as they are released from their "protected" and "sheltered" origin (the Earth), they come to meet us.

In this wooded place, Jardine describes an "ecological memory" that lives as a thread weaving him seamlessly into the *integrated curriculum* unfolding in the woods, where he is reminded of the place of his birth to which he now returns through "sensuous smells" (133). This "ecological memory" of which Jardine speaks is a revelation of the past in the present, and, in an important sense, it is also a remembering, or *remembrance*, or form of ontologically attuned thought, that foretells what is yet to be, intimating the potential *futural* state of education and curriculum. And, although this *presence* has not yet arrived, its prophetic ambience can be inhaled and *tasted* in the breath that "pulls this humid air," *felt* as the Earth underfoot bears us up, *heard* in the rustling of the leaves, the birds' songs, and "the rising insect drills of the cicada tree" (133). So intimate and complete is Jardine's "emplacement" in this once familiar dwelling-space, it is as if the place remembers him, for he states that "it feels as if this place itself has remembered what I have forgotten, as if my own memory, my own raising, some of my own, is stored up in these trees for safe keeping" (133). What is most important for Jardine, in this *remembrance*, is that he is not only relearning things, but learning anew from the Earth and its flora, fauna, fowl, and they show him things not merely "*about this place*," but as well about how he should "carry" himself when in all such kindred places, and beyond, how he should carry himself as an educator, how he should listen to the address of his students in the same way that he is now listening to the Earth's call. In nature, we learn of the heightened sense of responsibility and indebtedness that is required to "carry" ourselves in a "caring" manner, and part of "such carrying, such bearing," begins with learning "how the creatures of this place can become like great teachers" (135), thus we must be prepared to *become learners*.

Importantly, for Jardine, the lessons that the woodland creatures teach us are instantiated and grounded in the intuitive insight that "grasps" the integrity and value that always already antedates our *presence*, in an ontological sense, and this is one powerful instance of the potential of the re-awakening attunement from out of which we "learn" to approach the Earth and its inhabitants in ways, where in moments of transcendence, we responsibly assume the role of guardians, or as Heidegger indicates, *shepherds of Being.* However, it is really a form of co-guardianship in the sense that the Earth speaks first in that it opens the *originary* lines of communication necessary for all authentic "conversation." Reticently, but with great urgency, the Earth gives its demands, and, if authentic, we respond and enter into the "conversation" that demonstrates the "realization" that our "curriculum-of-life" is interwoven into the revealing and concealing of the Earth, within it *originary* and *poietic* "self-arising," which brings forth the world as a gift for our potential appropriation through its "unaided" *poietic* unfolding.

Jardine observes: "I slowly gathered something of this place, it became clear that I was also somehow 'gathering myself,'" and as "I gathered something of the composition of this place, I, too, had to become composed in and by such gathering" (136). This reciprocal conversation with the Earth and its creatures Jardine calls "gathering"—which indicates that as he remembered he simultaneously "learned" anew through this dialogue. To reiterate, as Jardine's words testify, this is not simply the remembrance of *what was*—it is also an instance that reveals *what might be* or more properly *what should be,* for this learning is both ontological and normative, and, as Jardine observes, "I *become* someone through what I know" (136), in other words, this learning as "emplaced transcendence" not only alters the way we are in the *present*, or the ways we will be in the *future*, it also changes forever the way we *have been,* for we have *become other* to ourselves in the "familiarity" of the dwelling-places grounded in primordial *otherness* and *mystery*. Jardine believes this form of learning in communion with the Earth is an essential and necessary "gift that environmental education can offer to education as a whole," and in its *essence*, learning occurs in and through transcendence, a change in attunement, an ontological "realization" that things have now changed, they are now *other,* and for Jardine, this re-awakening can be something as simple and yet deeply profound as "learning how to carry oneself in such a way that the ways of this place might show themselves. Education, perhaps, involves the invitation of children into such living ways" (136). He goes on to add that

> such a realization makes it possible to be at a certain ease with what you know. It is no longer necessary to contain or hoard or become overly consumptive in knowing. One can take confidence and comfort in the fact that this place itself will patiently hold some of the remembrances required: like the cicadas, patiently repeating the calls to attention required to know well of this place and its ways. (135)

And yet, as has been the running critique throughout, the insight arising from such "emplaced" encounters with the Earth cannot be expressed through ratiocination, through the logic of the syllogism, or through empirical data emerging from the application of one or another method or technique of quantitative research. But, it is not, for that reason, a learning that is insignificant. Quite the contrary, for this "knowing," this Earthen lesson as described, is "always and already deeply pedagogical, concerned not only with the living character of places, but with what is required of us if that living and our living there is to go on" (137). Jardine makes the point regarding phenomenological insight or understating eloquently in his description of an encounter with a "blue heron pair" that he spots flying overhead, and he shares the profound and wondrous experience of the recognition that in fact he "knows" *those* birds, *that* specific pair, from his prior walks down the woodland paths of his childhood. He claims that immediately, in a mode of *ek-static* transcendence, there was an inexplicable and "sudden rush of a type of recognition almost too intimate to bear, an event of birding never quite lodged in any birding guides" (139). And, what a marvelous, "strange and incommensurate piece of knowledge. How profoundly, how deeply, how wonderfully *useless* it is, knowing that it is *them*, seemingly calling for names more intimate, more proper than 'heron,' descriptions richer and more giddy" (139). Although it is proper to say that this knowing "doesn't lead anywhere," in terms of demonstrating the character of *instrumentality*, Jardine assures us that it is "by itself, always already full, always already enough" (139).

Epilogue

Magrini, James. M. *New Approaches to Curriculum as Phenomenological Text: Continental Philosophy and Ontological Inquiry.* New York: Palgrave Macmillan, 2015. DOI: 10.1057/9781137573186.0006.

I approach this brief epilogue in terms of "lingering in the *presence* of thought-worthy concerns." For in revisiting several of the reconceptualists who have contributed to *reading curriculum as phenomenological texts*, we learn that their themes and concerns are still relevant and very much alive in this contemporary age of standardized education, a time, when many follow the "scripted curriculum" for teaching students who are reduced to a "standard," a one-size-fits-all, lesson-plan grounded in educational research determining what is universally best and most profitable for all students, a standard that is already pre-determined before the first lines and activities of the lesson are spoken and enacted. Hence, we encounter standardized education as a rote exercise in ventriloquism. To break the hold or the attunement of empirical-analytic curriculum making, which *re-*presents world-*as-*picture, does not first require the alteration of our existing educational policies, although this would certainly represent an important later step in the process. Rather, as I have suggested, this calls for the turn from *epistemology* to *ontology* in our curriculum theorizing. If we take seriously the reconceptualists, then we become keenly aware of the human element that cannot be ignored in our institutionalized educational endeavors—the very type of *humanization* that the standardize curriculum ignores.

Thus we must ask, and this has always been Pinar's (1994) driving concern: What is the foundational view of the human being that underlies our methods and practices? What type of human being do our educational methods and practices endorse, but also, more importantly, inculcate, and beyond this, in an ominous manner, "create"? As I have shown, the human being that world-*as-*picture inculcates, as it is *re-*presented in scholarship and research of a scientific and empirical nature, is either a mechanistic and technological "product" or some form of "cognitive" processing unit, a brain *sans* body in a vat (or desk!) wired to electrodes apathetically awaiting stimulation from an external power source. Are these the only choices available to us, and beyond, are these limited views truly expressive of human autonomy and creative aesthetic development? Daignault (1992) reminds us, in line with the "abstract expressionist" scholarship of Pinar, that understanding curriculum is never reducible to capturing it as a phenomenon in a single view that is external to the unfolding of the educative activities: "Curriculum translation is always plural: WAYS; neither definite nor indefinite" (200). For example, the action-painting of Pollack, according to Pinar (1991), shows us that the human life unfolds within "everchanging landscapes," which always manifest "complexity" and, more often than not, a sense of "irrationality," and yet this instantiates, in an ontological manner, the "fullness" and fecundity of its immanent development and evolution (248).

Pinar's (2010) work, despite its expression through a multiplicity of permutations, continues to focus on the recurring question of the "subject" in curriculum studies. Importantly, as related to the concerns of this text, he notes that the constructed "character of the subject is in a sense fictional" (4). This indicates clearly that Pinar denies the conception of the *hypostatic* subject, or *subject as hypokeimenon*, where an essential substrate grounds "self-identity" and persists amid change. However, Pinar's conception of the subject should not be read as devolving into the "fictional" view of the subject found in certain strands of *post-modern* literature regarding the arbitrary and "non-existent" nature of the so-called "created social-subject," a view that has its *modern* origin in British empiricism, namely, in Hume's *bundle theory of mind against the substantial self.* For as Pinar states, the subject's "fictional character does not imply its insubstantiality or falsehood" (4). The most crucial aspect of this inquiry, which is concerned with the ontological aspects of education, curriculum, and learning, is the undeniable human, or better, "humane," aspects of curriculum and its conception, design, implementation, and evaluation. For even in the eco-phenomenology of both Jardine and Bonnett, there was a reconceived and de-centered view of the human emerging from our encounter with and analysis of nature and the Earth, which undoubtedly represents a "substantial" human *presence.*

What can educators and practitioners hope to draw form this text? Is there a way to formalize or concretize the findings in a way that is direct, succinct, and approachable? In response, I begin with Heidegger (1968) from *Discourse on Thinking,* and move to present four salient "talking-points" that relate what I have learned from my decade long engagement with the curriculum theorists working in phenomenology. Although the philosophical language I incorporate may seem to some "high flown" and "lofty," this is certainly not the case, and so I enlist Heidegger's assistance, who, much like Jardine and Bonnett, talks of the "rootedness" of phenomenological thought in and on the Earth. In fact I have dealt throughout and elsewhere with three major Heideggerian themes, several of which were merely intimated in the text, and they are *Gelassenheit* ("releasement"), *Inständigkeit* ("in-dwelling"), and *Bodenständikeit* ("autochthony/

rootedness"). In summation, we release ourselves over to phenomena in order to attempt to establish an authentic form of in-dwelling, in our case the in-dwelling is with others in the curriculum, and this requires a "rootedness" on the Earth, a return home, in terms of *Bodenständikeit* (autochthony). However, recalling Jardine's woodland vignette, it is clear that although the phenomenological themes are monumental in importance, their manifestation can occur in the most simple and mundane manner, e.g., in walking leisurely down a forest path, we feel the earth bear us up, offering its support, in a way that normally goes unnoticed, and yet for phenomenology, it is an occasion for the celebration of life for it inspires a sense of wonder (*thaumazein*). Heidegger makes a related observation on the primacy of attending to the so-called "mundane" aspects of our lives, which are those aspects that are actually closest to our Being, and we can do this because phenomenological thought shares an intimate bond with the Earth, and this form of *meditative* reflection

> need by no means be "high-flown." It is enough if we dwell on what lies close and meditate on what is closest; upon that which concerns us, each one of use, here and now; here, on this patch of home ground; now, in the present hour of history. (154)

The lessons learned, which include *earthen-lessons*, passed along from reconceptualist curriculum theorizing are here presented for the reader, but are not limited to the following:

(1) the reconceptualist approach to philosophizing both curriculum and education is unique: Papastephanou (2010) rightly observes, and this is a topic I introduced through Jardine, that in most contemporary philosophical approaches to education, education becomes the "object" of study. "In its *objective* sense the genitive 'of' constructs education as an *object* of philosophical endeavor. In doing so, it typically assigns education a subservient position and the status of a specialized region of inquiry" (451). What is typical in the field (and this includes some forms of *curriculum theorizing*) is the attempt to apply philosophy to education, e.g., philosophical topic X and education are "often approached by uncritically transferring established philosophical positions into education. The assumption is that issues of educational concern are compatible with, or adaptable to, ready-made philosophical categories," or vice versa (452). This is an approach that reconceptualist thought resists. Rather, they inspire an approach that lets "education" speak

in its own voice, to show itself in its own manner of self-showing by breaking open the "original" space of its appearance in our lives—"*apophainesthai ta phainomena* to let that which shows itself be seen from itself in the very way in which it shows itself from itself" (Heidegger, 1962, 58/34).

(2) Learning from reconceptualist thought we come to recognize the importance of the ways in which we view, talk, understand, and interpret both learning and the human being's relation to this original phenomenon, which is not an activity that is merely added on to our existence, but rather emerges through as made possible by unique Sense (*Sinn*)-making-giving structuring our *Being-in-the-world*. As stated, education in the age of standardization, is reliant on numbers, percentages, and statistics for the establishment of categories and classifications for what teachers need to know to be effective teachers, what students need to learn in order to be contributing members of the democratic society, and what an "efficient" performance and levels of "achievement" entail for both educators and students. Making such things our primary and exclusive concern exhibits the tendency to obscure the human, or *humane*, element in education, and this I have termed the *oblivion of ontology*. Reconceptualist thought presents us with a rich description of *phenomenological self-hood*, showing that the human being cannot be "leveled-down" or flattened-out in order to be cast into the one-size-fits-all die of "standardized" curriculum. There is more to the human being than can be captured in theories of a scientific or social scientific nature, in behavioral, cognitive, or neurological terms. Curriculum grounded in "scientific instrumentalism," as a metaphysical phenomenon, misses and occludes the unique and multifarious ways we express ourselves as dynamic and autonomous beings and the many and varied ways in which we are *in-the-world*.

(3) Reconceptualist curriculum has inspired my approach to the human in terms of an "original" learner, who by its very "nature" is always and already in the world (thrown-into-Being) as a primordial interpreter of its world (*hermeneuein*), which it shares with others in *Being-with-(Mitsein)-others-in-learning*. And this "origin" mode of learning, as *Being-in-the-world*, is bound inextricable to our *projection, understanding,* and *transcendence*, i.e., we are learning most originally when becoming *other* in the *presence*

of the *Other* (Magrini, 2014). Learning is about the wonder and potential of becoming something "new," becoming something *other* than we already are, and *that* we learn relating to *others* testifies that "learning" is never a solipsistic endeavor or *individuated* act of the closed off, interiorized subject. Rather, it is communal, and beyond, in terms of a "vocation," always already historical and temporal, i.e., learning is expressive of because it is the embodiment of our *historicity,* which is at once the dynamic unfolding of our Being, which might be grasped in terms of ecumenical acts of interpretation in the ever-renewed search for *meaning,* driven by the ontological *exigency* of the concern for our Being and the Being of others. Since our *Being-in-the-world* is irreducible to a linear conception of time, educators and those who design curriculum should be aware that the past must never be lionized and brought into the present in terms of the reified collection of social and cultural achievements to be aped or reproduced. Nor should the future be privileged in terms of the seeing of goals and ends of learning in advance of the processes of education's unfolding.

(4) Eco-phenomenology or the *ontology of nature* in Jardine and Bonnett teaches us that the Earth represents the supreme ontological *authority.* From the moment of "thrownness," our being born and jettisoned into the world that is not of our choosing, the Earth has already in advance claimed us, made its demands and placed upon us a supreme responsibility, which we can either accept and take up, in the face of its undeniable and obtrusive *presence,* or turn away from it. In *eco-phenomenology* as discussed, we encounter the immediacy and necessity of a return to an *originary* relationship with nature/Earth that was always present, which *metaphysical instrumentalism* has long since occluded. The lessons learned hold the revelatory and transformative power to change our relationship to education, to our children, and it begins, in terms of an *origin,* or new inception, with a "turning" back toward the Earth in all of its primordial sustaining power, which provides measure and guidance for a better life and concernful in-dwelling (*originary ēthos*), if we are prepared to release ourselves over to its call and address, and then allow our rejoinder to take shape from out of the unfolding of the reciprocal relations comprising our *curriculum-of-life* as it is set and nested within the context of the Earth's *integrated-curriculum.* Jardine (2000) states that it is necessary for educators to carry

transcendent encounters with the Earth home with them to the "often stuffy confines" of the classroom (140). The Earth grants and provides the revelatory "thread of kindredness with what one knows, a sense of deep relatedness and intimate, fleshy obligation," such that if we understand its address, we might, for the future of education and our children, allow it to inspire a change to the "literal-minded nature of academic work" (140), by ushering in renewed and *poietic* ways through which to authentically read, write, and speak in the present concerning the potential future of our educational and curricular practices.

My hope is that this book will inspire educators to consider alternative ways for conceptualizing learning and discoursing about it, in terms of a holistic, multifaceted, and irreducible phenomenon that outstrips rote instrumentalism and lives beyond the notion of the classroom as an "environment" within which the student is motivated and manipulated to perform certain behaviors or demonstrate specific cognitive skill-sets on cue, which are then assessed in terms of rising to or demonstrating the state of "learning." This I suggest, as is now evident to the reader, might be approached through the language of phenomenology, which, as stated, through the *poietic* process of "naming" anew, brings to language, brings to *presence*, the ontological aspects of our Being that have been covered over by the analytic-empirical language of contemporary standardized education. As I have suggested, phenomenological language, and the unique reconceptualization of phenomena it intimates, is perfectly suited to communicate the fluid, dynamic, and uncertain nature of the unfolding of our Being-in-*praxis* all the while preserving and sheltering the intangible, the *mysterious*, but no less invaluable for that reason, aspects of our existence relating to human *presence, historicity, temporality, transcendence, facticity,* and *finitude*. Language, as a *poietic* phenomenon, allows us to not only reconceive the world but it also offers the potential for us to appropriate the world in new and changed ways, to take an informed and authentic stand amid the unfolding of Being as the source of meaning within which we participate, facilitating and enlivening the ways we *live and learn*.

References

Anderson, L. & Krathwohl, D. (Eds.) (2001). *A taxonomy for learning, teaching and assessing: A revision of Bloom's taxonomy of educational objectives*. Thousand Oaks, CA: Corwin Publishers.

Anderson, T. (2006). *A commentary on Gabriel Marcel's the mystery of being*. Milwaukee, WN: Marquette University Press.

Aoki, T. (2005). *Curriculum in a new key: The collected works of Ted Aoki*. Mahwah, NJ: Lawrence Erlbaum Associates.

Barrett, W. (1960). *Irrational man: A study in existential philosophy*. New York, NY: Anchor Books.

Beardsley, M. (1965). *Aesthetics from classical Greece to the present*. Tuscaloosa, AL: University of Alabama Press.

Besmer, K., M. (2007). *Merleau-Ponty's Phenomenology*. New York, NY: Continuum.

Bonnett, M. (2015a). *Moral education and environmental concern*. New York, NY: Routledge.

———. (2015b). The powers that be: Environmental education and the transcendent. *Policy Futures in Education*, 13(1), 1–15.

———. (2013). Normalizing catastrophe: Sustainability and scientism. *Environmental Education Research*, 19(2), 187–197.

———. (2010). Education and selfhood: A phenomenological investigation. In: C. Ruitenberg (Ed.) *What do philosophers of education do? (And how do they do it?)* (41–53). Malden, MA: Wiley-Blackwell.

———. (2007). Environmental education and the issue of nature. *Journal of Curriculum Studies*, 39(6), 707–721.

———. (2004). *Retrieving nature: Education for a post-humanist age.* UK: Wiley-Blackwell.

Bransford, J. (2000). *How people learn.* San Francisco, CA: Jossey-Bass.

Brommer, G. (1988). *Discovering art history.* Worchester, MA: Davis Publications.

Brosio, R. (2000). Philosophical scaffolding for the construction of critical democratic education. New York: Peter Lang.

Critchley, S. (2010). Passive nihilism. *The Philosopher's Magazine*, 50, 36–37.

———. (2001). *Continental philosophy: A Short Introduction.* UK: London: Oxford University Press.

Daignault, J. (1992). Traces at work from different places. In: W. Pinar & W. Reynolds (Eds.) *Understanding curriculum as phenomenological and deconstructed text* (195–215). NewYork, NY: Teachers College Press.

Darling-Hammond, L. & Bransford, J. (2005). *Preparing teachers for a changing world.* San Francisco, CA: Jossey-Bass.

Dennett, D. (1991). *Consciousness explained.* Harmondsworth, UK: Penguin.

Dennett, D. (1990). *Consciousness explained.* UH: Back Bay Books.

Dreyfus, H. (2001). *Being-in-the-world: A commentary on Heidegger's being and time division I.* Cambridge: MIT Press.

———. (1999). The primacy of phenomenology over logical analysis. *Philosophical Topics*, 27(2), 3–24.

———. (1993). Heidegger's critique of Husserl's (and Searle's) account of intentionality. *Social Research*, 60(1), 1–13.

———. (1981). Knowledge and human values: A genealogy of nihilism, *Teacher's College Record*, 82, 507–520.

Freire, P. (1999). *Pedagogy of the oppressed.* New York, NY: Continuum Press.

Froman, W. (1993). Action painting and world-as-picture. In: G. Johnson (Ed.) *Maurice Merleau-Ponty's Aesthetics*, (337–347). Evanston, IL: Northwestern University Press.

Gelven, M. (1991). *Commentary on Heidegger's being and time.* DeKalb, IL: Northern Illinois University Press.

———. (1972). *Winter, friendship, and guilt.* New York, NY: Harper Torchbooks.

Gray, J. (2007). *Black mass: Apocalyptic religion and the death of utopia.* New York, NY: Farrar, Straus, and Giroux.

———. (2004). *Heresies: Against progress and other illusions.* Great Britain: Granata Books.

———. (2003). *Straw dogs.* New York, NY: Farrar, Straus, and Giroux.

Grumet, M. (1992). Existential and phenomenological foundations of autobiographical methods. In: W. Pinar & W. Reynolds (Eds.) *Understanding curriculum as phenomenological and deconstructed text,* (28–43). New York: Teachers College Press.

Grumet, M. & Pinar, W. (1976). *Toward a poor curriculum.* Berekely, CA: McCutchan.

Heidegger, M. (2015). *Holderlin's hymns "Germania" and the Rhine.* Bloomington, IN: University of Indiana Press.

———. (2001). *Contributions to Philosophy.* Bloomington, IN: Indiana University Press.

———. (1988). *Basic problems of phenomenology.* Bloomington, IN: Indiana University Press.

———. (1996). *Hölderlin's hymn the Ister.* Bloomington, IN: Indiana University Press.

———. (1993a). *Basic concepts.* Bloomington, IN: Indiana University Press.

———. (1993b). *Basic Writings.* San Francisco, CA: Harper-Collins.

———. (1977). *The question concerning technology and other essays.* New York, NY: Harper Torch Books.

———. (1971). *Poetry, language, thought.* New York, NY: Harper & Row.

———. (1968). *Discourse on thinking.* New York, NY: Harper & Row.

———. (1965). *History of the concept of time.* Bloomington, IN: Indiana University Press.

———. (1962). *Being and Time.* San Francisco, CA: Harper-Collins.

Howe, K. (2009). Epistemology, methodology, and education sciences: Positivist dogmas, rhetoric, and the educational science question. *Educational Researcher,* 38(6), 428–440.

Huebner, D. (1974). Remaking curriculum language. In: W. Pinar (Ed.) *Heightened consciousness, cultural revolution, and curriculum theory,* (8–26). Berkeley, CA: McCutchan.

———. (1966). Curricular Language and Classroom Meanings. In: J. Macdonald (Ed.) *Language and Meaning.* Washington DC: ASCD.

Jardine, D. (2000). *"Under the tough old stars": Ecopedagogical essays.* Brandon, BC: Solomon Press.

———. (1998). *To dwell with a boundless heart*. New York: Peter Lang.
———. (1992). Reflections on education, hermeneutics, and ambiguity. In: W. Pinar & W. Reynolds (Eds.) *Understanding curriculum as phenomenological and deconstructed text* (116–129). New York: Teachers College Press.
Jensen, E. (2005). *Teaching with the brain in mind*. Alexandria, VA: ASCD Press.
Kant. I. (1956). *Immanuel Kant's critique of pure reason*. New York, NY: St. Martin's Press.
Kelly, S. (2005). Closing the gap: Phenomenology and logical analysis. *The Harvard Review of Philosophy*, 13(2), 4–24.
Kirkland, S. (2013). *The ontology of Socratic questioning in Plato's early dialogues*. Albany, NY: SUNY Press.
Kliebard, H. (2004). *The struggle for the American curriculum*. New York: Routledge-Falmer.
Lovitt, W. (1977). *The question concerning technology and other essays*. (translator's introduction), xiii–xxxix. New York, NY: Harper Torchbooks.
Macdonald, J. (1995). *Theory as a prayerful act*. New York, NY: Peter Lang, 1–7.
Magrini, J. (2015). Phenomenology and curriculum implementation: Discerning a living curriculum through the analysis of Ted Aoki's situational practice. *Journal of Curriculum Studies*, 47(2), 274–299.
———. (2014). *Social efficiency and instrumentalism in education: Critical essays in ontology, phenomenology, and philosophical hermeneutics*. New York: Routledge.
———. (2012). Worlds apart in the curriculum: Heidegger, technology, and the *poietic* attunement of literature. *Educational philosophy and theory*, 44(5), 500–521.
———. (2010). The work of art and truth of being as "historical": Reading *being and time*, "the origin of the work of art," and the "turn" (Kehre) in Heidegger's philosophy of the 1930s. *Philosophy Today*, 54(4), 346–363.
———. (2009). "Anxiety" in Heidegger's *being and time*: The harbinger of authenticity. *Dialogue*, 48(2–3), 66–76.
Malewski, E. (2010). *Curriculum studies handbook*: The next moment. New York, NY: Routledge.
Marcel, G. (1995). *The philosophy of existentialism*. New York, NY: Citadel.
———. (1965). *Being and having*. New York, NY: Harper & Row.

———. (1950). *The mystery of being (Volume I)*. New York, NY: Gateway.
Matthews, E. (2003). *The philosophy of Merleau-Ponty*. Montreal, CA: McGill-Queen's University Press.
Merleau-Ponty, M. (1993a). Cezanne's doubt. In: G. Johnson (Ed.) *Maurice Merleau-Ponty's Aesthetics* (59–75). Evanston, IL: Northwestern University Press.
———. (1993b). Eye and mind. In: G. Johnson (Ed.) *Maurice Merleau-Ponty's Aesthetics* (121–149). Evanston, IL: Northwestern University Press.
———. (1993c). Indirect language and the voices of silence. In: G. Johnson (Ed.) *Maurice Merleau-Ponty's Aesthetics* (76–120). Evanston, IL: Northwestern University Press.
———. (1969). *The visible and the invisible*. Evanston, IL: Northwestern University Press.
McNeill, W. (1999). *Glance of the eye: Heidegger, Aristotle, and the ends of theory*. Albany, NY: SUNY Press.
———. (1996). *Holderlin's hymn "The ister,"* (translator's introduction). Bloomington, IN: Indiana University Press.
———. (2006). *The time of life: Heidegger and ethos*. Albany, NY: SUNY Press.
Morris, K. (2006). *Sartre*. UK: Oxford University Press.
Nietzsche, F. (1990). *Twilight of the idols*. UK: Penguin Group.
Nussbaum, M. (1990). *Love's knowledge*. New York: Oxford University Press.
Papastephanou, M. (2010). Method, philosophy of education and the sphere of the practico-inert. In: C. Ruitenberg (Ed.) *What do philosophers of education do? (And how do they do it?)* (131–149). Malden, MA: Wiley-Blackwell.
Pattison (2000). *The later Heidegger*. New York, NY: Routledge.
Pinar, W. (2013). *Curriculum studies in the United States*. New York, NY: Palgrave-Pivot.
———. (2010). *The worldliness of a cosmopolitan curriculum: Passionate lives in public service*. New York, NY: Routledge.
———. (1995). The reconceptualization of curriculum studies. In: D. Flinders & S. Thornton (Eds.) *The curriculum studies reader* (168–176). New York: Routledge.
———. (1994). *Autobiography, politics and sexuality*. New York: Peter Lang.
———. (1992). *Curriculum as phenomenological and deconstructed text*. New York, NY: Teachers College Press.

———. (1991). The white cockatoo. In: W. Schubert & G. Willis (Eds.) *Reflections from the heart of educational inquiry: Understanding curriculum and teaching through the arts* (244–249). Albany, NY: SUNY Press.

———. (1976). *Curriculum theorizing: The reconceptualists.* Berkeley, CA: McCutchan.

Puttfarken, T. (2003). Aristotle, Titian, and Tragic Painting. In: D. Arnold & M. Iversen (Eds.) *Art and thought: New interventions in art history.* UK: Blackwell Publications.

Quinn, C. (2009). Perception and painting in Merleau-Ponty's thought. *Perspectives:International Postgraduate Journal of Philosophy,* 2 (1), 9–30.

Rouse, J. (2001). Coping and its contrasts. *Division I faculty publications.* Paper 39. http://wesleyan.edy/divIfacpubs/39.

Sartre, J-P. (1989). *Being and nothingness.* London: Routledge.

Sartwel, C. (1992). *A companion to aesthetics.* UK: Wiley-Blackwell.

Searle, J. (1998). *Mind, language and society.* New York: Basic Books.

———. (1983). *Intentionality: An essay in the philosophy of mind.* Cambridge: Cambridge University Press.

Schiro, M. (2009). *Curriculum theory: Conflicting concerns and enduring visions.* Los Angeles: Sage.

Schubert, W. (1991). The speculative philosophical essay. In: E. Short (Ed.) *Forms of curriculum inquiry* (61–76). Albany, NY: SUNY Press.

Stewart, D. & Mickunas, A. (1990). *Exploring phenomenology.* Athens, OH: Ohio University Press.

Taubman, P. (2009). *Teaching by numbers.* New York: Routledge.

Thomson, I. (2009). Environmental Philosophy. In: M. Wrathall & H. Dreyfus, *A companion to phenomenology and existentialism* (445–463). UK: Wiley-Blackwell.

Tyler, R., W. (1950). *Basic principles of curriculum and instruction.* Chicago, IL: University of Chicago Press.

Vallega-Neu, D. (2013). Heidegger's Poietic writings: From *Contributions to Philosophy* to *Das Ereignis*. In: J. Powell (Ed.) *Heidegger and Language* (146–162). Bloomington, IN: Indiana University Press.

———. (2001). Poietic Saying. In: D. Vallega-Neu, C. Scott, et al. *Commentary on Heidegger's Contribution to Philosophy* (66–80). Bloomington, IN: Indiana University Press.

Vandenberg, D. (1975). Openness: The pedagogic atmosphere. In: D. Nyberg (Ed.) *The philosophy of open education*, (135–147). London, England: Routledge & Kegan Paul.

———. (1974). Phenomenology and educational research. In: D. Denton (Ed.) *Existentialism and phenomenology in education* (183–220). New York: Teachers College Press.

———. (1971). *Being and education: An essay in existential phenomenology.* Englewood Cliffs: Prentice-Hall.

Van Manen, M. (2014). *Phenomenology of practice: Meaning-giving methods in phenomenological research and writing.* Walnut Creek, CA: Left Coast Press.

Van Manen, M. (1990). *Researching lived experience.* Albany, NY: SUNY Press.

Willis, G. (1991). Phenomenological inquiry: Life-world perceptions. In: E. Short (Ed.) *Forms of curriculum inquiry* (173–186). Albany, NY: SUNY Press.

———. (1975). Curriculum criticism and literary criticism. *Journal of Curriculum Studies,* 7(1), 3–17.

Wittgenstein, L. (1958). *Philosophical investigations.* Oxford: Wiley-Blackwell.

Young, J. (2001). *Heidegger's philosophy of art.* Cambridge, MA: Cambridge University Press.

Index

absorbed coping, 18, 29–31, 33, 42
abstract expressionism, 46, 51, 55, 60, 63, 66, 70
abstract expressionist scholarship, 46–9, 65, 66, 69, 73–4, 112
achievement, 12–13, 19, 25, 115–16
action painting, 46, 51, 55, 60, 63–6, 68, 73, 112
AERA (American Educational Research Association), 49, 54
aesthetic phenomenon, 46, 60
aesthetics, 51, 55, 57, 59–60, 72, 78
aletheuein, 11, 14, 58
Aoki, Ted, 4, 19, 27–8, 42
art
    action-painting, 46, 51, 55, 60, 63–6, 68, 73, 112
    anti-metaphysical, 60, 71
    metaphysical, 55, 57–9, 64
    non-metaphysical, 46, 57, 60, 71
Auseinandersetzung, 5, 6

Being-educated, 34–8
Being-in-the-world, 26, 28–9, 31, 33, 43, 60, 63, 66, 69–70, 74, 95, 105–6, 115–16
Bonnett, Michael, 4, 78

eco-phenomenology, 77, 113, 116
emplaced transcendence, 105–7
humanism, 80–3
nature as "self-arising" phenomenon, 77, 95–104
breakdown-and-revelation, 29–30, 32

Cezanne's art, 60–2, 72
chaos, 87–9
cognitive knowledge, 22, 27, 42, 50
Common Core State Standards Curriculum, 12, 20, 52
concept empiricism, 7, 25, 35, 36, 46, 50
conceptual knowledge, 25, 27, 29, 42
criterion of correctness, 10, 61
critical pedagogy, 12, 82
Critique of Pure Reason (Kant), 78
cultural framing, 96, 106
curriculum
    earthen-lessons, 114–17
    eco-pedagogy, 86–95
    fundamental educational theory, 33–42
    integrated curriculum-of-life, 86–95, 108–9, 116
    occluded ontology in standardized, 20–6

curriculum – *continued*
  phenomenological
    reconceptualization of world and human, 26–33
    reading of, as phenomenological texts, 2–3, 8, 18, 112
    reconceptualist thought, 6–8, 74–5, 114–15
  reconceptualization of, 7, 25, 46
  rootedness on Earth, 113–14
  simulacra of, 66–7, 97
  thinking-writing, 3, 4, 8
curriculum vitae, 68, 73, 77, 90–1

Descartes, Rene, 28, 51, 55, 58, 78, 81
Diagnault, J., 66, 97, 112
dialogical method, 38–41
dialogic principle, 18, 37, 40
directionality
  epistemological, 79–80, 85, 87, 90
  Nature/Earth, 83
  ontological, 85, 86, 87
dis-closure
  modes of, 47–9, 74
  world, 49, 51–2, 55–6, 72
Discourse on Thinking (Heidegger), 113
Dreyfus, Hubert, 4, 13, 18
  absorbed coping, 18, 29–31, 33, 42
  human subject, 43–4
  intentional action, 24–5
  objectifying practices, 26–33
  original learning, 41

Earth, 94–5
  attuned educational experience of nature, 104–10
  ecopedagogy and curriculum-of-life, 86–95
  eco-phenomenology, 15, 77, 113, 116–17
  nature as self-arising phenomenon, 77, 95–104
  ontological mystery, 88–9, 94–5
  post-humanist view of de-centered phenomenological subject, 78–86
  rootedness in curriculum, 113–14
ecological awareness, 83, 86
ecopedagogy, 77, 83, 87, 89
  integrated curriculum-of-life and, 86–95
eco-phenomenology, 15, 77, 113, 116–17
education
  achievement, 12–13, 19, 25, 115–16
  attuned educational experience of nature, 104–10
  Being-educated, 34–8
  call of phenomenology, 19–20
  grounding of ground, 42–4
  human being, 7–8, 11, 16, 18, 20–1, 27–8, 112–13, 115
  lessons learned, 114–17
  nature as self-arising phenomenon, 77, 95–104
  occluded ontology of contemporary standardized curriculum, 20–6
  standardized, 11–12, 18, 20–1, 27, 29, 49, 51–2, 70, 112, 117
emotional intellection, 27
emplaced transcendence, 77, 105–7, 109
En-framing, 51–2, 58, 60
epistemological directionality, 79–80, 85, 87, 90
epistemological mystery, 100
epistemology, 18, 28, 31, 35, 37, 42, 44, 78, 83, 86, 100, 112
ēthos, 84–5, 116
everyday activity, 29, 32, 36, 39, 57–8
exigency, 105, 116
existence, is-ness of, 35, 42–3
existentialism, 7, 12, 83

factual knowledge, 27, 42
First Critique, Kant, 78–9
fundamental educational theory, 33–44
  grounding of ground, 42–4
  principles of, 37–8
fundamental ontology, 7, 28, 33, 69

Greene, Maxine, 4

Index

Heidegger, Martin, 3–7, 11–12, 14, 18–19, 25, 46–7
  Being in Time, 34
  concept of Earth, 94–5
  Continental philosophy of, 77
  description of *physis*, 94, 101
  Discourse on Thinking, 113
  En-framing, 51–2
  fundamental ontology, 28
  Gelassenheit, 107
  human Being-in-the-world, 43
  humanism, 80–1, 83–5
  interpretation of Plato, 26
  meditative thought, 90
  metaphysical art, 58–9, 62, 64, 66
  ontological transcendence, 30–3
  phenomenology, 36, 39–40
  philosophy of "fourfold", 92–3
  poietic phenomenon, 66, 68–72, 74
  science-as-research, 50–4
  shepherds of Being, 108
  themes, 113–14
  tool-Being, 29
  world-as-picture, 48–9, 55–6, 97
hermeneutic interpretation, 34–6, 38–9, 69
hermeneutic phenomenology, 35, 42, 69
Hölderlin's poetry, 59–60, 92–4
Huebner, Dwayne, 3, 4, 7
human being
  Being-educated, 34–8
  education, 7–8, 11, 16, 18, 20–1, 27–8, 112–13, 115
human existence, 3, 16, 28, 37, 41, 73, 83, 85
humanism
  post-, 77, 80–1
  secular, 80–2
humanization, curriculum, 7, 112
Hume, David, 61, 78, 113

ICBM (Three-Year Integrated Competency-Based Model), 51
impressionism, 61

instrumentalism, *see* metaphysical instrumentalism
integrated curriculum-of-life (curriculum vitae), 68, 73, 77, 90–1, 108–9, 116
intentionality, 24, 29, 41

Jardine, David, 4, 28
  analysis of Kant, 78–80
  eco-pedagogy, 77, 83, 85–6, 86–95
  eco-phenomenology, 77, 113, 116
  emplaced transcendence, 77
  nature, 98, 100, 105, 107–10, 114
  phenomenological subject, 82–3
Journal of Curriculum Theorizing (journal), 8, 9

Kant, Immanuel, 61, 78–81, 104
Kelly, Sean, 4, 13, 18, 29, 33
Klee, Paul, 63, 64
knowledge, 27
  chaos, 87–9
  cognitive, 22, 27, 42, 50
  conceptual, 25, 27, 29, 42
  factual, 27, 42
  metacognitive, 22, 27, 42
  procedural, 23–4, 27, 29, 42

language, 3, 113
  art, 46, 49, 60, 62
  curriculum, 91
  nature, 96–7
  painterly, 46, 49, 66, 68, 71, 74
  painting, 65–6
  phenomenology, 10–11, 117
  poietic, 66–75
learning sciences, 18, 20–2, 29, 52–4
lessons learned, curriculum, 114–17
"lived" curriculum (curriculum vitae), 68, 73, 77, 90–1, 108–9, 116
lived experience, 7–9, 13, 15, 18, 23, 28, 31–2, 35–6, 38–9, 55, 60, 62, 97, 102, 104

Macdonald, James, 4, 5, 7, 9, 12

McNeill, William, 4, 6, 10, 13, 53–4, 70, 74–5
Marcel, Gabriel, 4, 77, 88–9, 97, 105–6
mathematics/mathemata, 51, 52, 56, 81–2, 88, 91–2, 96–7
meaningfulness, 15
meditative thought, 11–13, 90, 114
Merleau–Ponty, Maurice, 4, 28, 46
  aesthetics, 51, 55
  art, 48, 60–6
  "painterly" expression, 66, 68, 71–2, 74
metacognition, 20, 22, 27
metacognitive knowledge, 22, 27, 42
metaphysical art, 55, 57–9, 64
metaphysical instrumentalism, 2, 12
  abstract expressionist scholarship, 66–75
  action-painting, 65
  art re-presenting, 58, 65, 71
  attunement of, 96, 98
  epistemological directionality of, 90
  ontological mystery, 88
  relationship with nature/Earth, 77, 78–86, 90, 116
  science-as-research, 50
  technical re-presentation of, 51–7
  world-as-picture, 48, 50, 51–7
metaphysics of mastery, 78, 82, 96, 98, 107
mutual anticipation, 106–7

nature
  attuned educational experience of, 104–10
  eco-phenomenology, 15, 77, 113, 116–17
  physis, 69, 94, 101
  post-humanist view of de-centered phenomenological subject, 78–86
  self-arising phenomenon, 77, 95–104
  storytellers, 107–8
  value of, 101–3, 105–8
No Child Left Behind, 12
non-ideational intentionality, 29, 41
non-metaphysical art, 46, 57, 60, 71

objectification, 13, 26, 49
objectifying practices, 25, 26, 62, 67–8
ontological, 15
ontological ecology, 87, 89
ontological mystery, Earth/Being, 88–9, 94–5
ontological transcendence, 30, 104
original learning, 28, 38, 41
originary learning, 15

painterly language, 46, 49, 66, 68, 71, 74
painting
  academic, 61
  action, 46, 47, 51, 55, 60, 63–6, 68, 73, 112
  art of, 47–9, 62–3, 72–3
  Cezanne, 60–2, 72
  expressive language of, 65, 68
  Renaissance, 55–7
passive nihilism, 80
pathmarks for learning, 38
phenomenological self-hood, 18, 28, 115
phenomenological subject, 21, 25, 77, 78, 82–3
phenomenology
  call of, 19
  criterion of correctness, 10, 61
  eco-phenomenology, 15, 77, 113, 116
  metaphysicalization of, 13
  practice of, 3
  reconceptualization of world and human, 26–33
philosophy, terminology of, 15–16
physics, 69, 94, 101
Pinar, William, 3, 4, 35, 60, 62
  abstract expressionist scholarship, 46–51, 66–75, 112–13
  curriculum theory, 7–9
Plato, 14, 26, 34, 58, 59, 61
poietic language, phenomenology, 11, 66, 69–71, 74
Pollack, Jackson, 46–8, 63–4, 73, 112
post-humanism, 77, 80–1
primal mystery, 11, 13–15, 69
primordial mystery, 15, 84, 87, 100, 104

problem-based learning, 23
procedural knowledge, 23–4, 27, 29, 42
proto-phenomenology, 14

Race to the Top, 12
reading of curriculum as phenomenological text, 2–3, 8, 18, 112
re-awakening (re-attunement), 77, 83, 88, 92, 103, 105, 107–9
reconceptualization
 curriculum, 7, 25, 46
 education, 25, 33, 35–6
 phenomena, 117
 world and human, 26–33
referential totality, 30, 32–3
reification, 13, 42, 66–7, 71, 116
Renaissance art, 51, 54–7, 64, 81
re-presentational research, 46–51
Rouse, Joseph, 28, 30

Sartre, J.-P., 10, 12, 83–5
Schubert, W., 8–10
science-as-research, 50–6
science of learning, 20–6
scientific method, 23–4
scientism, 50, 82, 96, 99, 106–7
secular humanism, 80–2
self-inquiry, 67, 68
self-knowledge, 67
sense (Sinn), symbolic, 59
Sense (Sinn)-giving/making structures
 phenomenological method, 36, 38–40
 transcendence, 105
 understanding of, 14–16, 18, 115
simulacra of curriculum, 66–7, 97
social efficiency, 18, 19, 21, 25, 41–3, 107
speculative philosophical essay, 3, 8, 9
standardized curriculum, occluded ontology of, 20–6

standardized education, 11–12, 18, 20–1, 27, 29, 49, 51–2, 70, 112, 117
STEM education, 20, 52
sustainable development, 87, 98–9, 105
system of relations, 31–2

taxonomy, new, for learning, 2, 23, 27
thinking, meditative, 11–13, 90, 114
thinking-writing, curriculum, 3, 4, 8
thought experiments, 23–4
transcendence, 15, 97, 106–10
transcendental, 16
transcendental idealism, 79
truth-happening, 8, 66, 101
 art, 58, 64, 74
 dis-closure, 52, 74
 events of, 47–9, 65

universal invariant structures, 13–14, 16

Vallega-Neu, Daniela, 4, 10–11, 13, 69–71
Vandenberg, Donald, 4, 12
 fundamental educational theory, 33–44
 phenomenology of education, 18–20
van Manen, Max, 4, 7, 9–10, 13, 16, 19

White Cockatoo, The (Pollock's action-painting), 46, 47
"The White Cockatoo" (Pinar essay), 46
Willis, George, 10, 13–14, 19
will to power, 78, 82, 99
Will to Power as Art (Heidegger), 6
world-as-picture, 11, 13, 48, 50, 81, 97
 action painting, 64
 age of, 51–7, 60
 art re-presenting, 58–60
 curriculum, 66–70, 112

GPSR Compliance

The European Union's (EU) General Product Safety Regulation (GPSR) is a set of rules that requires consumer products to be safe and our obligations to ensure this.

If you have any concerns about our products, you can contact us on

ProductSafety@springernature.com

In case Publisher is established outside the EU, the EU authorized representative is:

Springer Nature Customer Service Center GmbH
Europaplatz 3
69115 Heidelberg, Germany

www.ingramcontent.com/pod-product-compliance
Lightning Source LLC
LaVergne TN
LVHW041956060526
838200LV00002B/35